Eyewitnesses
To American
Jewish History

Edited by

AZRIEL EISENBERG

HANNAH GRAD GOODMAN

UNION OF AMERICAN HEBREW
CONGREGATIONS · New York

EYEWITNESSES TO AMERICAN JEWISH HISTORY

A History of American Jewry

PART I · From the Colonial Period
Through the Revolution · 1492-1793

CONTENTS

Foreword   vii

1. CHRISTOPHER COLUMBUS Announces His Discovery to Santangel, 1493   3

2. JUAN DE TORQUEMADA Reports on the Inquisition in the Americas, 1574–1593   9

3. A DUTCH JEW Visits a Jewish Colony Founded in Surinam in 1632   12

4. A TREASURER Forwards the First Contribution from the New World to the Holy Land, 1637   17

5. AMSTERDAM JEWS Plead for the Jews of Recife, 1645   20

6. JACQUES DE LA MOTTE Brings 23 Jews to New Amsterdam, 1654   25

7. THE COURT Hears a Case against Abram De La Simon, 1655   27

8. THE DUTCH WEST INDIES Company Intervenes for the Jews, 1655–1656   29

9. BARBADOS JEWS Receive a Torah Scroll from Amsterdam, 1657   32

10. THE NUÑEZ FAMILY Flees from Lisbon, 1732   35

11. A NEW YORK CONGREGATION Engages a Hazan, 1757   39

12. NEW YORK JEWS Respond to an Appeal from Safed, 1761   44

13. MOSES MICHAEL HAYS Protests a Loyalty Oath, 1776   47

14. MORDECAI SHEFTALL Recalls His Capture by the British, 1778   49

15. JAMES MADISON Writes about Haym Salomon, 1782   55

16. BENJAMIN RUSH Attends a Jewish Wedding, 1787   59

· v ·

17. JONAS PHILLIPS Writes to the Federal Constitutional Convention, 1787   63

18. MANUEL JOSEPHSON Advises the Newport Congregation, 1790   67

19. NAPHTALI PHILLIPS Recalls the Federal Parade of 1788   70

20. EMMA LAZARUS Visits the Newport Synagogue, Abandoned in 1791   74

21. A GERMAN JEWISH SETTLER Writes about Life in Virginia, 1792   78

22. JOHN TRUMBULL Tells How David Franks Came to His Defense, 1793   83

FOREWORD

EYEWITNESSES TO AMERICAN JEWISH HISTORY is the second in our series published by the Union of American Hebrew Congregations. The gratifying reception to the first volume, *Eyewitnesses to Jewish History: From 586 B.C.E. to 1967*, is evidence of the acceptance of the eyewitness approach. To quote from the Foreword of the first book, "History textbooks of necessity consist of highly condensed, emotionally-dehydrated generalizations. They are important in presenting . . . facts and for providing summaries. . . . They cannot transmit the emotional impact and tone of a happening. The eyewitness approach of on-the-spot stories adds flesh to the dry skeleton of history and infuses it with life and spirit. It gives new meaning to facts, imparts insights and attitudes, provides a mood, conveys an emotional impact."

The second book will appear in four parts, divided according to the organization suggested by Professor Jacob R. Marcus, the distinguished historian of American Jewish history. His periodization of the subject falls into four divisions: (1) Colonial Period and Sephardic Immigration; (2) German Immigration; (3) Eastern European Immigration; and (4) the American Jew. These four parts will be published separately and then will appear in a single cloth-bound volume.

In preparing this, the first section, we are deeply grateful to *Publications of the American Jewish Historical Society* from which we drew many quotations. We acknowledge our thanks to the Society and to the other publications for their courtesies in permitting us to reprint the selections that follow. We are also indebted to *American Jewish Archives* and libraries and museums that have furnished us with documentary photographs and permission to reprint them.

We are pleased to acknowledge our thanks to the late Dr. I. E. Kiev, chief librarian of the Hebrew Union College-Jewish Institute of Religion, and his staff and to Mr. Harry J. Alderman, chief librarian of the American Jewish Committee, and his staff for the many courtesies they afforded us in the preparation of this work.

We are grateful to Mr. Abraham Segal, erstwhile director of the Commission on Jewish Education, and to Rabbi Daniel Syme, its acting director, for their interest and encouragement; to Mr. Ralph Davis and his associates, Mrs. Josette Knight and Mrs. Annette Abramson, who saw the book through the press; to Miss Patricia Pierce who typed the manuscript. Finally, we express our special thanks to Dr. Jacob R. Marcus who has been generous in responding to our queries.

The two books in this series, published by the Union, are designed for schools and study circles as well as for leisure home reading. To assist the teacher or group leader, comprehensive teachers' guides have been published and are available on order from the UAHC.

A.E.

H.G.G.

Eyewitnesses
To American
Jewish History

CHRISTOPHER COLUMBUS
Announces His Discovery to
Santangel, 1493

As one of the last vessels carrying Spanish Jews into exile sailed up the Atlantic coast, it passed a little fleet leaving in search of a new world. The admiral commanding the three caravels was a Genovese whom we know as Christopher Columbus.

Thus, as the history of the Jews in Spain came to an end, the history of the Jews in America began.

It is not chance that the Jews were expelled from Spain and Columbus's voyage was launched in the same year. On March 31 of 1492, the Catholic monarchs gave the Jews four months to leave. The decree was made public on April 30, the same day that Columbus was ordered to equip a fleet for the Indies. On August 2, some 300,000 Jews left Spain; the next day Columbus set sail.

At that time Aragon's comptroller-general was Luis Santangel, a Marrano (secret Jew) whose uncle had died at the stake in Saragossa. Together with Ferdinand's chamberlain, Juan Cabrero, also of Jewish lineage, Santangel had approached Isabella in Columbus's behalf; he had also given money for the expedition. It was to Santangel and to the treasurer of Aragon, the Marrano Gabriel Sanchez, that Columbus sent first word of his discovery.

The voyages were financed "not by jewels but by Jews" seeking refuge from rack and stake—partly through confiscated properties, partly by contributions. The first contributor was Isaac Abravanel who, in 1483, had fled from Portugal to Spain for safety.

A number of Jews sailed with Columbus: the interpreter Luis de Torres, the surgeon, the physician, and several crewmen. Columbus took with him the astronomical tables of Abraham Zacuto, the noted Jewish mathematician—a gift of the Jew Joseph Vecinho, physician to King João II of Portugal.

Columbus's letter to Santangel, excerpted here in translation from the Spanish, is obviously intended also for royal eyes.

"... In twenty days I reached the Indies. ..."

SIR, SINCE I knew that you will take pleasure at the great victory with which Our Lord has crowned my voyage, I write this to you. In twenty [actually thirty-three] days I reached the Indies with the fleet which the most illustrious King and Queen, our lords, gave to me. And there I found very many islands filled with people without number, and of them all I have taken possession for Their Highnesses. To the first island which I found I gave the name *San Salvador* in remembrance of His Heavenly Majesty. . . . To the second I gave the name of *Isla de Santa Maria de Concepcion;* to the third, *Ferrandina;* to the fourth, *La Isla Bell* [a misprint of Isabella]; to the fifth, *La Isla Juana.* . . .

When I reached Juana, I followed its coast to the westward, and I found it to be so long that I thought it must be the mainland. . . . And, since there were neither towns nor cities on the coast but only small villages, with the people of which I could not have speech because they all fled forthwith, I went forward . . . thinking that I should not fail to find great cities and towns. And, at the end of many leagues . . . I sent two men upcountry to learn if there were a king or great cities. They traveled for three days and found an infinite number of small villages. . . .

I understood sufficiently from other Indians . . . that this

| Tab eclipſis luminariuȝ et primo de ſole | | | | | | | | |
numer⁹ annornȝ	nomina menſiuȝ	dies	digiti	feria	hore	minut	finis eclipſis hore	minu
1493	octob	10	9	5	0	0	1	20
1502	ſepteb	30	8	6	17	28	19	12
1506	Julii						3	3
1513	martii						1	9
1518	Juni						9	17
1524	Januar						4	6
1494	ſepteb						2	33
1497	Januar						7	18
1500	noueb						8	30
1501	maii						9	6
1502	octob						2	9
1504	februa						4	13
1505	aug⁹							6
1508	Junii							0
1509	Junii							3
1511	octob	6	13	2	9	11	2	25
1514	Januar	29	15	2	14	20	16	3
1515	Januar	19	15	7	5	0	6	42
1516	Julii	13	14	1	10	0	12	30
1519	noueb	6	20	1	5	50	6	48
1522	ſepteb	5	15	6	11	22	12	4
1523	martii	1	17	1	7	30	9	14

Authentic reproduction of an early portrait of Columbus. (Spanish Government Office of Information) The background is from the Almanac of Abraham Zacuto (1450-1515) whose astronomical tables were used by Columbus on his voyage. (Jewish Theological Seminary of America/Darmstaedter) land was an island, and so I followed its coast eastwards one hundred and seven leagues up to where it ended. And from that cape I saw another island, distant eighteen leagues . . . to which I at once gave the name *La Española*. . . . In it there are many harbors and numerous rivers, good and large, which is marvelous. Its lands are lofty and in it there are many sierras and very high mountains . . . and filled with trees of a thousand kinds and tall, and they seem to touch the sky; and I am told that they never lose their foliage. . . . Upcountry there are many mines of metals. . . . *La Española* is marvelous, the sierras and the mountains and the plains and the champaigns and the lands are so beautiful and fat for planting and sowing. . . . The harbors are such as you could not believe it without seeing them, and so the rivers, many and great, and good streams, the most of which bear gold. . . .

The people all go naked, men and women . . . except that some women cover one place only. . . . They have no iron or steel or weapons, nor are they capable of using them, although they are well-built people of handsome stature, because they are wonderfully timorous. They have no other arms than canes . . . to the ends of which they fix a sharp little stick; and they dare not make use of these, for oftentimes I have sent ashore two or three men . . . and, as soon as they [the people] saw them coming, they fled; even a father would not stay for his son; and this not because wrong has been done to anyone; on the contrary, I have given them of all that I had, such as cloth and many other things, without receiving anything for it; but they are like that, timid beyond cure. It is true that, after they have been reassured and have lost this fear, they are so artless and so free with all they possess that no one would believe it. . . . Of anything they have, if you ask them for it, they never say no; rather they invite the person to share it and show as much love as if they were giving their hearts; and . . . they are content with whatever little thing may be given to them. I forbade that they should be given things so worthless as pieces of broken crockery and broken glass, and ends of straps, although they thought they had the best jewel . . . a sailor for a strap received gold to the weight of two and a half *castellanos*, and . . . for new *blancas*, for them they would give all that they had, although it might be two or three *castellanos'* weight of gold or an *arrova* or two of spun cotton . . . so that it seemed to me to be wrong and I forbade it, and I gave them a thousand good, pleasing things which I had brought. . . . And they know neither sect nor idolatry, with the exception that all believe that the source of all power and goodness is in the sky, and they believe very firmly that I, with these ships and people, came from the sky. . . . And this does not result from their being ignorant, for they are of a very keen intelligence and men who navigate all those seas, so that it is marvelous the good account they give of everything, but because they have never seen people clothed or ships like ours.

And as soon as I arrived in the Indies . . . I took by force some of them in order that they might learn [Castilian] and give me information . . . ; they soon understood us, and we them, either by speech or signs, and they have been very serviceable. I still have them with me, and they are still of the opinion that I come from the sky . . . and they were the first to announce this wherever I went, and the others went running from house to house and to the neighboring towns with loud cries of "Come! Come! See the people from the sky!" . . . and all brought something to eat and drink, which they gave with marvelous love. In all the islands they have very many *canoas* like rowing *fustes* . . . and some are bigger than a *fusta* [large rowboat] of eighteen benches. They are not so broad, because they are made of a single log, but a *fusta* could not keep up with them by rowing, since they make incredible speed, and in these [canoes] they navigate all those islands. . . . Some of these canoes I have seen with seventy and eighty men in them, each one with his oar. . . .

In all these islands, it appears, all the men are content with one woman, but to their *Majoral,* or king, they give up to twenty. It appears to me that the women work more than the men. I have been unable to learn whether they hold private property, but it appeared true to me that all took a share in anything that one had, especially in victuals.

In conclusion, to speak only of that which has been accomplished on this voyage, which was so hurried, Their Highnesses can see that I shall give them as much gold as they want if Their Highnesses will render me a little help; besides spice and cotton; and gum mastic, . . . and aloe wood . . . and slaves, as many as they shall order. . . . And I believe that I have found rhubarb and cinnamon, and I shall find a thousand other things of value. . . . And the truth is I should have done much more if the ships had served me as the occasion required. . . .

So, since our Redeemer has given this victory to our most illustrious King and Queen, and to their famous realms, in so great a matter, for this all Christendom ought to feel joyful and make great celebrations and give solemn thanks. . . .

Done in the caravel off the Canary Islands, on the fifteenth of February, year 1493.

At your service.

The Admiral

From the *Spanish Newsletter,* September 30, 1964,
Embassy of Spain Information Department,
translated by Samuel Eliot Morison

JUAN DE TORQUEMADA Reports on the Inquisition in the Americas, 1574-1593

The Inquisition relentlessly pursued the Jews into the New World. It brought its regime of terror and torture to the Spanish and Portuguese colonies in South and Central America.

The Portuguese tracked down Marranos (secret Jews) in the Americas and shipped them back to Lisbon for trial. The Spanish, however, set up courts of the Inquisition on American soil, and Jews were martyred here for their faith as early as 1574 and as late as the early nineteenth century. In fact, the Inquisition records, which are a saga of Jewish heroism, are among the best sources of information on early Jewish migrations to the Americas.

The history of the Inquisition on these shores is one long, sad, and bloody tale of spies and extortion, of torture chambers and racks, of agonized women forced to betray their husbands and of children tortured into revealing their parents, and of cruel death. Execution was usually by an *auto de fe* which literally means "act of faith" but actually was death at the stake.

Juan de Torquemada, a monk who may have been related to the Tomás de Torquemada who founded the Inquisition, leaves us an enthusiastic eyewitness account of some of these proceedings. His book, *Indian Monarchy*, published in 1723, reports that, in nineteen years (1574 to 1593), nine *autos de fe* were held in the colonies. In the first alone, there were sixty-three "penitentials" of whom five were burnt alive. Sixty victims were rounded up in 1596, over one hundred in 1602.

Torquemada saw these grisly affairs as things of

beauty. His ferocity and his uncomplicated enjoyment of them are revealed in the following excerpt from *Indian Monarchy*.

". . . And each had a monk by his side who exhorted him to die well."

THE PLACE selected was the town hall, being in the principal square of the city, where was ordered to be erected a sumptuous seat . . . above which was the canopy of the tribunal, which with its silk curtains and the beautiful worked and rich carpets . . . made a most majestic appearance.

It was quite a marvelous thing to see the people who crowded to this celebrated and famous *auto;* they were in the windows, and every place, which they filled, and even to the house and doors of the Holy Office; and to see the singular procession . . . of the relaxed and penitentials who came out with ropes about their necks and pasteboard caps on their heads, with flames of fire painted on them, in their hands they held a green cross, and each had a monk by his side who exhorted him to die well; they had also familiars of the Holy Office for a guard. The reconciled Jews with *sambenitos*, those twice married with caps, upon which were painted objects signifying their crimes. Those accused of witchcraft with white caps on their heads, candles in their hands, and ropes about their necks. Others for blasphemy, with gags in their mouths, half naked, their heads uncovered, and with candles in their hands . . . ; those for lesser crimes going first, and in the same order the rest, the relaxed following behind, and the dogmatists and teachers of the Law of Moses as captains or leaders, the last with their trains on their caps, rolled up and twisted to signify the false doctrines they taught, and in this manner they proceeded towards the place erected for them, in front of the seats for the tribunal. . . .

As for the scaffold, or framework for the seats of the condemned, it was marvelous, because in the middle of it was a half pyramid, surrounded by semicircular steps up to the top; upon these were seated in their order the relaxed, the dogmatists upon the highest steps, and the others in gradation, and in this order also were the effigies of those who were relaxed but who were either dead or absent. The reconciled and other penitentials were seated upon low benches in the open space of the scaffold. The head jailor of the Holy Office had a chair placed for him at the base of the scaffold, a pulpit was also placed upon the right of the Holy Office, from which a sermon was preached by the Archbishop of the Philippine Islands, Don Frai Ignacio de Santi-vañes, of the order of my glorious father San Francisco. Two other pulpits were placed, one on each side of the tribunal, from which were read . . . the sentences of the condemned . . . ; it will be enough to say that there were many of those obstinate Jews, who each one might have been a rabbi of a synagogue. All this was celebrated with great majesty . . . the people not being a little astonished at the rites and ceremonies, as well as at the enormous crimes . . . of these Judaizing heretics.

From *Indian Monarchy*, by Juan de Torquemada, 1723, Vol. III, p. 379, as quoted in *Publications of the American Jewish Historical Society*, Vol. LIV, 1964–65, pp. 164–166

A DUTCH JEW Visits a Jewish Colony Founded in Surinam in 1632

As far as we know, the first white settler in the New World was a Jew. Luis de Torres, Columbus's interpreter, settled in Cuba and there lived out his days. In the next century a few other intrepid Jews, in their desperate search for a place where they could live and practice their religion in peace, found their way to the West Indies; and it is known that Jewesses who had been forcibly baptized were shipped there by Spain.

Jews were reported in Barbados as early as 1628, and when the French occupied Martinique in 1635 they found Jews already there.

In 1644, exiled Spanish and Portuguese Jews who had taken refuge in Holland were sent to Curaçao by the Dutch. By 1650 the island boasted twelve Jewish families who had been provided with land, slaves, horses, cattle, and farming implements. This small Jewish community increased in numbers and wealth and still exists today.

Many of the Jews who fled from the Dutch colonies in Brazil in 1654, when the Portuguese captured Recife, escaped to the West Indies.

England was so eager for West Indian colonies that she promised that Jews who settled in Surinam would be regarded as British-born. In 1632 a small group went to the island where they enjoyed full religious freedom. The fortunes of war brought Surinam into Dutch hands, but the little community of Jews continued to prosper.

Two centuries later, a Dutch Jew visited the remains of one of the colonies in Surinam. His notes, translated from the Dutch, give us an idea of the peaceful haven it had once afforded the Jews who settled there.

"Everything was rotten, decayed, and mouldering."

THE SAVANNA [plain] of the Jews is an insignificant village or hamlet, being the property and the late residence of Portuguese Jews. * * * Situated in the division of upper Surinam, ten hours or so, or two days navigating from Paramaribo . . . on the river Surinam.

Herewith follows an abstract of my journal of voyages:

And now we are shown the picturesque hillock upon which stands a synagogue built of stone. In front of this quiet hamlet in the middle of the river, lies a charming *tabbetje* or uninhabited island * * * completely overgrown with trees, shrubs, and bushes. . . .

Before one reaches the green hillock . . . one sees at the foot of it various military buildings. . . . Here resides the commanding officer of the military post Gelderland which is behind the hamlet, and he has here his picket.

Not less attractively located is the village which is built upon the hill around the synagogue . . . ; its grave stillness arouses serious and reverential feeling and reminds us of bygone times and manners.

                ❅   ❅   ❅   ❅   ❅

This village should be looked at only from a distance. Everywhere you meet oppressing poverty upon the ruins of former prosperity, there are only a few senile, decrepit Israelites in the dilapidated houses, surrounded by decayed ruins. . . . The evening we spent . . . in the most prominent house of this village, with Mr. T. de la Parra in the company of a few good, old people . . . Jews of between seventy and eighty years of age who communicated to us . . . the original and early privileges which they enjoyed here, while they complained . . . about the loss of their own private jurisdiction. Also prophesied those hospitable men, who stood with one foot already in their graves . . . that after death their residences like so many others would be deserted and uninhabited.

Their ancestors, according to their story, arrived here as fugitives in consequence of the persecution in Spain and Portugal, having received permission from our government [the Netherlands] in 1632. . . .

The synagogue was erected in the year 1685, which last date stands upon the iron pillar near the westerly gable-wall . . . and is situated on a high, spacious square . . . being the level summit of a hill . . . above the river. The synagogue itself, surrounded by a wooden railing, painted black, is erected entirely of bricks and is a very strong building with two pointed gables, with stoops on both sides, without steeple or clock-work. . . . Inside is a wooden arch supported by pillars of genuine brown hard-wood. At the westerly end is a gallery . . . containing the seats for the women; below this gallery one finds three apartments, in one of which sat the tribunal of the Jews. This privilege they obtained from Queen Anne of England. . . . However, this court of justice . . . together with various other privileges, has expired and was abolished by royal decree, d.d. 7 April, 1825, on July 4, 1825.

In the apartment to the left, besides the fire-engine there are today a large chest of books and other archives. Here a number of children are instructed during divine service. To the east stands the sacristy; a large chest contains, upon eighteen scrolls, the books of Moses, each of these scrolls comprehends the *Penta-teuch*, written on vellum in Hebrew; the sticks, upon which these holy laws and teachings are rolled, have a splendid crown of silver and gold, while each of these eighteen scrolls is wrapped in a variously flowered silken covering. On the north side are seats of the officers. . . . The quantity of copper crowns and

chandeliers is witness to the former prosperity of this community; these were gifts of prominent Jews, whose names are en-
graved upon them. . . .

On October 12/13, 1785, the Jews celebrated the centennial
jubilee of this synagogue; more than 1,600 persons are said to
have attended this . . . magnificent festival, amongst whom were
the Governor-General Wichers, the Police Counsellors, and Civil-
Counsel, Staff Officers, and various high officials. . . .

. . . We turned to the southeast corner of the square to visit
an old coffee-house; but this dilapidated hovel . . . was uninhabited and locked up. There were a great number of vermin,
and . . . everything was rotten, decayed, and mouldering. . . .

Close by the billiard house we partook of a collation with Da
Costa, and we promenaded eastwards to the so-called village . . .
to the cordon of the military post. . . . There were upon this
oblong square once about eighty·to ninety houses, but in 1790
it must have been well nigh a deserted wilderness, as there were
then living, in forty-nine houses, only twenty-two miserable inhabitants, and, in October, 1822, not more than eight. . . .

. . . Many prominent Portuguese Jews established themselves
here only to be buried at this cemetery with their ancestors. The
former prosperity of this hamlet had its origin in the trade
necessary to the supply of the former strong garrison of the
cordon * * * which now is almost deserted . . . for which reason the trading Israelites removed from here and settled in
Paramaribo. . . .

To the right . . . is situated the Jewish cemetery with a great
number of marble tombstones on which are Hebrew inscriptions.

*   *   *   *   *

After breakfast we concluded . . . to visit the cemetery of the
old Jews . . . ; we were able to reach the same by water in
half an hour. . . . Upon the first high cliff stood the old Jewish
synagogue before the year 1685. . . . Ere long we reached the
old cemetery of the Jews, where you find an abundance of

tombstones which have more the shape of a prism than of an oblong square . . . scattered in every direction. . . . In the middle of this solitary, lonely cemetery stood a stately, black tree which overshadows with its broad crown the silent graves. . . .

From *De Landbouw in de Kolonie Surinamen*,
by M. D. Teenstra, 1835,
as quoted in *History of the Jews of Surinam*,
by Richard Gottheil, pp. 135–141

A TREASURER Forwards the First Contribution from the New World to the Holy Land, 1637

Wherever the Jews wandered in their long search for ground beneath their feet, they remembered Zion. Their love for the ancient homeland of their people never wavered.

The Spanish and Portuguese Jews had a burning love for *Terra Santa,* the Holy Land. Some of the greatest poetry expressing the Jewish yearning for *Eretz Yisrael,* the Land of Israel, was written by the twelfth-century Spanish poet, Judah Halevi. It was the custom of Spanish Jews to leave bequests to one of the struggling Jewish communities in *Eretz Yisrael.* After the expulsion from Spain, many Jews made their way to Palestine, bringing about a renaissance of Jewish culture in the Holy Land in the sixteenth century.

In Recife, too, on the distant continent of South America, the exiled Jews remembered the land of their fathers. In 1637 a treasurer in Amsterdam received a contribution from that remote outpost to which fate had taken a group of Portuguese Jews—the first contribution on record from the New World to the Land of Israel. He accepted the contribution—some of it in the form of sugar—and forwarded it to Venice where other helping hands would speed it on its way to the four holy cities—Jerusalem, Safed, Tiberias, and Hebron. The letter describing the transaction is given here, in translation from the Portuguese, with its apparent miscalculations.

From then on, the Jews of Brazil sent regular contributions through the Amsterdam community. In appreciation, the *parnassim* (trustees) of the Amsterdam synagogue offered a special prayer for the Recife Jews every Yom Kippur eve. The episode shows the strong bond that existed among the scattered Jewish communities.

". . . Since Jerusalaim has the two boxes [of sugar] that arrived from Brazil. . . ."

IN AMSTERDAM the 13th of *Jaar* [*Iyar*] of 5399 Years [May 17, 1639]. An account of the money that is now being sent to *Terra Santa* through Mr. Abraham Aboaf of Venice, the distribution of which was made by the gentlemen who served the past year as Deputies of the Nation, such being money promised in its time.

There was for the general [distribution in the] Holy Land the following:

In the hand of Mr. Aaron Maestro	f	440:1
In the hand of Mr. Dauid Espinosa	f	138:11½
In the hand of Mr. Josuah Jesurao Roiz, and Ab. Farar for Bet Jahacob	f	537:28½
In the hand of Mr. Mikael Espinosa, who was temporary treasurer for the Holy Land	f	150:0
Mr. Dauid Ergas gave voluntarily five rixdalorsz [Reichs dollars]	f	12:10
Total	f	1,279:10

Said f 1,279:1 are divided as appears below.

For Safed with respect to the *Siluhijm* [emissaries] who went to Venice and since Jerusalaim has the two boxes [of sugar] that arrived from Brazil	f	636:10
For Jerusalaim f 432:11 for the above reason	f	432:11
For Hebron f 140	f	140:0
For Teberijah f 70.0	f	70:0
Total	f	1,279:1

For Jerusalaim

From the f 1,279:1 for the Holy Land, there is due it	f	432:11
From Abraham Farar for Bet Jahacob	f	73:5
From Dauid Curjel, who was administrator	f	220:0
From the two boxes of sugar [that] arrived from Brazil, net after freight and costs and other expenses, there remains exactly	f	330:0
From Abraham Franco Mdez. [Mendez], temporarily f 160 and whatever more there may be, there remains on credit	f	160:0
Total	f	1,215:16

From the *Livro dos Acordos*, p. 13,
as reproduced in *American Jewish Archives*,
January, 1955, pp. 36–37

AMSTERDAM JEWS Plead for the Jews of Recife, 1645

As early as 1548, Jews were banished to Brazil by the Portuguese. In that year, sugar cane, transplanted from Madeira, was introduced into Brazil by Portuguese Jews.

They still could not practice their faith openly for Inquisition agents operated in Brazil. When Portugal fell to Spain in 1580, the Inquisition ruled in both lands, and the Marranos in Brazil lived in an atmosphere of suspicion, hate, and dread.

In the early seventeenth century, almost all merchants of Jewish extraction were arrested. Then a list of Jews in Brazil, with "the most precise information on their properties," was drawn up—boding ill for the Neo-Christians, as they were called.

Jews rejoiced, therefore, at Dutch plans in 1617 to conquer Brazil; and the Dutch counted on their help. The Dutch West Indies Company was formed in 1622 to further these colonial ambitions.

In 1624 the city of Bahia was captured by the Dutch who proclaimed freedom of religion. Many Marranos threw off their masks and lived openly as Jews. But the Portuguese retook Bahia a year later, and the treaty between Holland and Portugal protected all inhabitants but the Neo-Christians. Abandoned by the Dutch, a number were put to death. Nonetheless, the Jews remained loyal to the Netherlands.

When the Dutch took Recife (Pernambuco) in 1631, Bahia's Jews hastened there, and others from Holland joined them. Settled mainly by Jews, Recife became the great center of Brazil's Jewry.

The Portuguese, scandalized at the synagogues in Recife, plotted to retake the city. The Jews got wind of the plans and frantically warned the Dutch.

This is the setting of the next selection in which Amsterdam Jews appeal to the mayors of Amsterdam to protect their brethren if Recife should fall, lest they suffer the fate of Bahia's Jews. The Dutch wrote to the consuls in Brazil that same day.

"... With tears of blood running from their hearts...."

November 27, 1645

THE JEWISH Nation, living in this town of Amsterdam, humbly requests that your Honors kindly show compassion toward them on account of the miserable state that the occurrences in Brazil have brought about.

Your Honors well know . . . , when the first ambassador of the present King of Portugal came to these countries, . . . he brought with him full powers from his king to grant various privileges and favors to the Jewish Nation, by this means seeking to persuade them to return to his countries and Kingdom. . . . Thereupon the [Jewish] Nation gave as their answer that they knew as their sovereign no one else but their High Mightinesses [of the States-General of Holland]. . . .

Of this, your Honors were then informed and . . . were requested kindly to make special mention of this to their High Mightinesses, the States [-General], so that, in the event any agreements might be concluded with the said king(s), their High Mightinesses should kindly remember this [Jewish] Nation with the purpose of having them . . . considered in the same manner as the other burghers and residents. . . .

The special favor which they received from His Highness [their High Mightinesses, the States-General] has aroused the unspeakably great hatred of the Portuguese against the [Jewish] Nation. This hatred has grown even more fierce since our people in Brazil had the opportunity to discover and to warn the

Recife, Brazil, 17th century, a painting by Zachariah Wagener, courtesy, Library of Congress. (American Jewish Archives)

A diorama depicting the arrival of the first Jews in North America at New Amsterdam, September, 1654. (American Jewish Archives)

[Netherlands] Government about the treacheries of the Portuguese a long time before they actually took place. The Portuguese were thereupon so embittered . . . that they publicly proclaimed that no quarter would be given to our Nation. Already they have executed in cold blood thirteen persons whom they had captured and, as is said, have burned one alive.

Your Honors may please consider that this hate and enmity keep on multiplying on account of the loyalty and vigilance with which the Jews . . . truly try to defend Brazil. For this end they expose their lives at considerable danger(s), as is shown by the fact that now more than forty persons volunteered for service in the Armada to fight against her [the Netherlands'] enemies. And, unlike other nations, no one of the [Jewish] Nation, God be praised, has been swayed, either by gifts or promises, to run away.

Such is the extremity of the peril . . . that suppliants are compelled to address themselves to your Honors, with tears of blood running from their hearts, humbly requesting that your Honors, by favorable letters . . . to their High Mightinesses, the States [-General], . . . will effect their issuing to the Government of Brazil an order so firm and so forceful that they shall be obliged by express order, on all occasions and at all times that any agreements with the enemy may be concluded, to consider and hold the Jewish Nation like the other inhabitants and subjects of their High Mightinesses, without any difference whatsoever, and so to include and treat them. In addition, to grant them your special favor as well as boats and good passage, should they, . . . singly or with their families and belongings, wish to return to these lands, especially since . . . for them there exists no quarter.

For these reasons, in the event of danger, heaven forbid, the Nation should be the first to be saved. The word of the enemy is not to be trusted since . . . they do not keep it, as demonstrated when they put to death the thirteen [Jews].

We hope that . . . the good advice of your Honors will induce their High Mightinesses, in their mercy, to . . . protect the many souls that the enemy wants to oppress and exterminate; to bring about the restitution of the goods of their loyal subjects; and also to grant relief to the many families, widows, and orphans who, under the good and fatherly protection of their High Mightinesses, had brought their belongings there [Brazil]. . . .

God always rewards those who have acted kindly towards this poor, dispersed Nation.

In concluding, [your] suppliants pour out of their hearts and the depths of their souls the words of Queen Esther to King Ahasuerus, viz, "If it please the king, give me my life—that is my petition! Grant me my people—that is my request!" (Esther 7:3). . .

From *The State Archives* at The Hague,
as quoted in *American Jewish Archives,*
January, 1955

JACQUES DE LA MOTTE Brings 23 Jews to New Amsterdam, 1654

Early in September of the year 1654, a small boat named the *Sainte Catherine* sailed into the harbor of New Amsterdam, the Dutch colony that later became New York City. Aboard it were 23 Jews fleeing from Recife, Brazil, which had recently fallen to the Portuguese. They had come via the West Indies.

On September 7, Jacques de la Motte, captain of the *Sainte Catherine,* submitted to the New Amsterdam Court of Burgomasters and Schepens (city officials) a petition in French requesting payment of 2,500 florins for passage of the Jews from Cape St. Anthony in Cuba to New Amsterdam.

While the sum seems high, and the Jews had probably been despoiled of their valuables, they had had no choice but to accept the terms. In the trial which followed, it was brought out that, shortly, they expected funds from Holland.

The authorities ordered that their property be sold and that two of them be imprisoned until the sum was paid in full.

This was not a good start for the newcomers. Peter Stuyvesant, the governor of New Netherlands, an ill-tempered and bigoted man, ordered the fugitives to leave. Before his order could be carried out, however, instructions came from the West Indies Company, many of whose directors were Jewish, that the newcomers were to stay. For the moment, at least, the 23 were safe.

Jacques de la Motte's request is still in the records of New York City. A translation of it follows.

".... There are 23 souls, big as well
as little, who must pay equally."

J ACQUES DE LA MOTTE, captain of the bark named *St. Cath-rien*, requests by a petition (written in French) the payment for the freight and food of the Jews brought here from Cape St. Anthony, according to agreement and contract, by which each is individually bound; and that therefore the furniture and whatever else the Jews have aboard his bark may be publicly sold by order of the Court towards the payment of their debt. It was orally declared that the Netherlanders who came over with them are not included in the contract and have satisfied him. Salomon Pietersz, a Jew, appeared in Court and said that nine hundred and odd guilders of the 2,500 f[lorins] have been paid and that there are 23 souls, big as well as little, who must pay equally. The petition and the contract having been seen by the noble Court, it is decreed that, according to the contract, the Jews shall pay that which remains of their debt within twice twenty-four hours after date, and meanwhile the furniture and whatever else is in the hands of the petitioner should remain as security without alienating the same.

From *The Records of New Amsterdam from 1653–1674*,
as quoted in *Publications of the American Jewish*
Historical Society, Vol. XLIV, 1954–55, p. 87

THE COURT Hears a Case against Abram De La Simon, 1655

The claim of Jacques de la Motte against his passengers seems to have been settled satisfactorily, for there is no record of further proceedings against the 23 Jews. Soon after, their number was augmented by the arrival of another group from Holland, Jews of greater means.

Their situation was precarious, however. They did not receive the welcome they had apparently expected from the Dutch colony; the expectation of that welcome must have prompted them in the first place to go to New Amsterdam from the West Indies. Their presence was barely tolerated by Peter Stuyvesant and some of his associates.

When one of the Jews, Abram De La Simon, made a slip, the consequences were dire. In February of 1655, De La Simon, who observed the Sabbath on Saturday, had kept his shop open on Sunday, the Christian Sabbath. He was immediately arrested. When the charge was read against him, the Portuguese-speaking defendant did not even understand what his crime had been.

Nonetheless, the error afforded an excuse to demand the eviction of the hapless group from the colony.

The charge against De La Simon, in translation from the Dutch, appears below.

"*. . . That the Jews who came here last*
year . . . must prepare to depart forthwith. . . ."

Monday, 1st March, 1655
In the City Hall

PRESENT: The Heeren Allart Anthony, Oloff Stevenson, Cornelis Van Tienhoven, Johannes Verbrugge, Johannes Nevius, Johannes de Peyster, Jacob Striker, and Van Vinge.

Cornelis Van Tienhoven, in quality of Sheriff of this City, Plaintiff, vs. Abram De La Simon, a Jew, Defendant.

Plaintiff rendering his demand in writing, saying that he, De La Simon, hath kept his store open during the Sermon and sold by retail, as proved by affidavit, concluding, therefore, that Defendant shall be deprived of his trade and condemned in a fine of six hundred guilders. The charge having been read before Defendant, who not understanding the same, it was ordered that a copy be given Defendant to answer the same before next Court Day. The Herr Cornelis Van Tienhoven informed the Burgomaster and Schepens that the Director General and Supreme Council have resolved that the Jews who came here last year from the West Indies, and now from Fatherland, must prepare to depart forthwith, and that they shall receive notice thereof, and asked if the Burgomasters and Schepens had anything to object thereto. It was decided, not; but that the resolution relating thereto should take its course.

From *Valentine's Manual for 1849,*
as quoted in *Publications of the American Jewish*
Historical Society, Vol. 1, 1893

THE DUTCH WEST INDIES COMPANY Intervenes for the Jews, 1655-1656

Bill of Rights for Jews

The Jews had to fight for their rights from the moment they landed here. Hunted and despoiled, with few doors open to them, they clung desperately to their foothold on these shores.

Peter Stuyvesant's ire rose at news that expected from Holland were other Jews who would "then build here a synagogue." He ordered the newcomers to leave, but orders to the contrary arrived from the Dutch West Indies Company which had Jewish investors and directors.

The Jews remained, but they were not to build a synagogue, open retail stores, or be employed in the public service. They were to care for their own poor—a point on which Stuyvesant need not have worried since they already had such a directive from the *Torah*.

The restrictions had important consequences: Jews were forced into foreign and intercolonial commerce. With exiled brothers all over the world, they were able to become importers and exporters, developing the colonies' foreign trade.

Some Jews had to return to the West Indies to make a living. Others are believed to have left in 1655 for Rhode Island where the liberal Roger Williams had guaranteed that "all men may walk as their conscience persuades them, every one in the image of his God." Actually, Williams's religious freedom was intended for persecuted Christians. His colony did admit Jews but refused them citizenship.

The Jews who remained fought steadily for dignity and normalcy. The earliest was Polish-born Asser Levy, the only Ashkenazic [German or Western] Jew among the 23 Jewish arrivals, who finally won the right to do guard duty.

In the following letters to Peter Stuyvesant, translated from the Dutch, the Dutch West Indies Company states its position on the Jews in no uncertain terms.

———————

". . . Provided the poor among them shall not become a burden to the Company or to the community but be supported by their own nation."

26th of April, 1655

W E WOULD have liked to agree to your wishes and request that the new territories should not be further invaded by people of the Jewish race for we foresee from such immigration the same difficulties which you fear, but, after having further weighed and considered this matter, we observe that it would be unreasonable and unfair, especially because of the considerable loss sustained by the Jews in the taking of Brazil, and also because of the large amount of capital which they have invested in shares of this Company. After many consultations we have decided and resolved upon a certain petition made by said Portuguese Jews, that they shall have permission to sail to and trade in New Netherland and to live and remain there, provided the poor among them shall not become a burden to the Company or to the community but be supported by their own nation. You will govern yourself accordingly.

✿   ✿   ✿   ✿   ✿

13th of March, 1656

The permission given to the Jews to go to New Netherland and enjoy the same privileges as they have here [in Amsterdam] has

been granted only as far as civil and political rights are con-
cerned, without giving the said Jews a claim to the privilege of
exercising their religion in a synagogue or a gathering; so long,
therefore, as you receive no request for granting them this liberty
of religious exercise, your considerations and anxiety about the
matter are premature, and, when later something shall be said
about it, you can do no better than to refer them to us and await
the necessary order. . . .

        ✿   ✿   ✿   ✿   ✿

14th of June, 1656

We have seen and heard with displeasure that, against our
orders of the 15th day of February, 1655, issued at the request
of the Jewish or Portuguese nation, you have forbidden them to
trade to Fort Orange and the South River, also the purchase of
real estate, which is granted to them without difficulty here in
this country, and we wish it had not been done and that you
had obeyed our orders which you must always execute punctually
and with more respect: Jews or Portuguese people, however, shall
not be employed in any public service (to which they are neither
admitted in this city), nor allowed to have open retail shops, but
they may quietly and peacefully carry on their business as afore-
said and exercise in all quietness their religion within their
houses, for which end they must without doubt endeavor to
build their houses close together in a convenient place on one
or the other side of New Amsterdam—at their choice—as they
have done here.

From *Documents Relating to the Colonial History
of the State of New York*, Vol. XIV,
as quoted in *Publications of the American Jewish
Historical Society*, Vol. 1, 1893, pp. 47–48

BARBADOS JEWS Receive a Torah Scroll from Amsterdam, 1657

"The Jews, who are connoisseurs of valuables," wrote Heinrich Heine, "knew very well what they were about when, in the conflagration of the Second Temple, they left the gold and silver vessels of sacrifice, the candelabra and lamps, even the High Priest's breastplate with its large jewels, and rescued only the *Torah*. This was the real treasure of the Temple."

The Jews were well aware of the value of their treasure. Wherever they were scattered, they carried it with them, cherished it, and guarded it.

When they made their way to the strange and distant lands across the Atlantic, it was not long before the *Torah* was there, too. Several of the Jews who left Amsterdam for Brazil in 1633–34 brought their own precious scrolls with them. The Amsterdam *parnassim* [trustees], who had encouraged their fellow Jews to migrate to the Dutch colonies and later to the French and English islands, provided them with Torah Scrolls and sacred ornaments.

The first Jewish settlers in New Netherlands received a *Torah* in 1655 but had to return it in 1663 because they did not have a *minyan* (a quorum for services).

In 1657 two Portuguese leaders accepted a pair of Holy Scrolls for delivery to the Jewish community in Barbados. The transaction was carefully recorded, as is seen in the following selection translated from the Portuguese. Apparently the *Sefer Torah* never reached its destination for a second one was sent to the same congregation in September of that year.

Facsimile of the introductory page to Bradford's "History of the Plymouth Plantation." (Contemporary Jewish Record, November-December, 1937)

From the introduction to the Bay Psalm Book, 1640, the first book published in the New World. The early books in colonial America reflected strong Hebraic influences through biblical references and the use of the Hebrew language. (Library, Jewish Theological Seminary of America)

Preface.

members, but the whole Church is commanded to teach one another in all the severall sorts of Davids psalmes, some being called by himselfe מִזְמוֹרִים: psalms, some תְּהִלִּים: Hymns some שִׁירִים: spirituall songs. soe that if the singing Davids psalmes be a morall duty & therfore perpetuall; then wee under the new Testamēt are bound to sing them as well as they under the old: and if wee are expresly commanded to sing Psalmes, Hymnes, and spirituall songs, then either wee must sing Davids psalmes, or else may affirm they are not spirituall songs· which being penned by an extraordinary gift of the Spirit, for the sake especially of Gods spirituall Israell; not to be read and preached only (as other parts of holy writ) but to be sung also, they are therefore most spirituall, and still to be sung of all the Israell of God: and verily as their sin is exceeding great, who will allow Davids psalmes (as other scriptures) to be read in churches (which is one end) but not to be preached also, (which is another end foe their sin is crying before God, who will allow them to be read and preached, but seeke to deprive the Lord of the glory of the third end of them, which is to sing them in christian churches. obj. 1 If it be sayd that the Saints in the primitive Church did compile spirituall songs of their owne inditing, and sing them before the Church. 1 Cor. 14, 15, 16.
Ans. We answer first, that those Saints compiled these spirituall songs by the extraordinary gifts of

* 3   the

"... A Sefer Torah of fine parchment. ..."

WE, ABRAHAM Chillão [*sic*] and Abraham Mesiah, declare that we received from the gentlemen of the *Mahamad* a *Sefer Torah* of fine parchment with its yellow taffeta lining; a band of red damask; a cloak of green and red satin with gold lace border; a cloth of green camel hair with white flowers for the reading desk, and *senifa* of mottled blue; some curtains of green damask with fringes; a flowered satin cloth of dark red and white to cover the *Sefer* at the reading desk; two *remonim* of gilt wood, and a box containing the Holy Scroll and all what has been given to us for delivery to the Island of Barbados to our brethren there who, at the behest of this K.[ahal] K.[adosh], shall . . . pay what the gentlemen of the *Mahamad* may ask. Amsterdam, the 16 *Yar* [*Iyar*] of 5417 [April 29, 1657].

(signed) Abraham Chillon

From the *Portuguese Jewish Archives*,
as quoted in *American Jewish Archives*,
January, 1955, p. 19

THE NUÑEZ FAMILY Flees from Lisbon, 1732

When Governor James Oglethorpe left England for the newly-chartered colony of Georgia, forty Marranos sailed with him. They reached Savannah on July 11, 1733, a month after it was founded. With them they carried a *Sefer Torah* (Scroll of the Law), an *Aron Kodesh* (Ark of the Law), and a box containing circumcision instruments.

Among them were Dr. Samuel Nuñez and his family who had escaped from the Inquisition in Lisbon the year before. Several members of the distinguished Nuñez family had died at the stake for their religion, and two had been sentenced to the galleys for life, but still the family was steadfast to the faith of their fathers. Samuel Nuñez, though court physician, had been arrested for heresy, and his family had been imprisoned. Because Nuñez's medical services were needed, they were released, but two officers of the Inquisition lived with them to keep an eye on their religious practices.

They had arranged their escape under the very noses of the two Inquisition spies who, one bright day in 1732, unexpectedly found themselves sailing down the Tagus River and out to sea. The story of the Nuñezes' escape is told in this selection.

Free at last to worship according to their conscience, the Jewish community in Georgia immediately founded a synagogue, Mikveh Israel (Hope of Israel). With a dozen German Jewish families who joined them shortly after, they were one-third of the colony's population. The colony's trustees at first refused to grant them any land, and Samuel Nuñez almost left; later he was granted six farms. One of his descendants was the

noted statesman, Manuel Mordecai Noah of New York.
The first white male child born in Georgia (July 7, 1734) was Philip Minis, son of Portuguese-born Abraham Minis and his wife Abigail.

". . . The brigantine shot out of the Tagus, was soon at sea, and carried the whole party to England."

THE DOCTOR had a large and elegant mansion on the banks of the Tagus, and being a man of large fortune he was in the habit of entertaining the principal families of Lisbon. On a pleasant summer day he invited a party to dinner, and among the guests was a captain of an English brigantine anchored at some distance in the river. While the company were amusing themselves on the lawn, the captain invited the family and part of the company to accompany him on board the brigantine and partake of a lunch prepared for the occasion. All the family, together with the spies of the Inquisition and a portion of the guests, repaired on board the vessel; while they were below in the cabin enjoying the hospitality of the captain, the anchor was weighed, the sails unfurled, and, the wind being fair, the brigantine shot out of the Tagus, was soon at sea, and carried the whole party to England. It had been previously arranged between the doctor and the captain who had agreed for a thousand moidores [a former Portuguese coin worth about $3.27] in gold to convey the family to England and who were under the painful necessity of adopting this plan of escape to avoid detection. The ladies had secreted all their diamonds and jewels which were quilted in their dresses; the doctor, having previously changed all his securities into gold, it was distributed among the gentlemen of the family and carried around them in leathern belts. His house, plate, furniture, servants, equipage, and even the dinner cooked for the occasion were all left and were subsequently seized by the Inquisition and confiscated to the state. On the

דִּקְדּוּק   לְשׁוֹן   עִבְרִית   *N° 271.*

DICKDOOK LESHON GNEBREET.

A

G R A M M A R

OF THE

𝔥𝔢𝔟𝔯𝔢𝔴 𝔗𝔬𝔫𝔤𝔲𝔢,

BEING

An E S S A Y

To bring the 𝔥𝔢𝔟𝔯𝔢𝔴 𝔊𝔯𝔞𝔪𝔪𝔞𝔯 into 𝔈𝔫𝔤𝔩𝔦𝔰𝔥,

to Facilitate the

I N S T R U C T I O N

Of all thofe who are defirous of acquiring a clear Idea of this

Primitive Tongue

by their own Studies ;

In order to their more diftinct Acquaintance with the SACRED ORACLES of the Old Teftament, according to the Original.   And

Publifhed more efpecially for the Ufe of the STUDENTS of *HARVARD-COLLEGE* at *Cambridge*, in NEW-ENGLAND.

נֶחְבַּר וְהוּגַת בְּעִיּוּן נִמְרָץ עַל יְדֵי
יְהוּדָה מוֹנִישׁ

Compofed and accurately Corrected,

By J U D A H   M O N I S, *M. A.*

B O S T O N, N. E.

Printed by JONAS GREEN, and are to be Sold by the AUTHOR at his Houfe in *Cambridge*.   MDCCXXXV.

A Grammar of the Hebrew Tongue, the first Hebrew grammar printed in America, 1735. The author, Judah Monis, teacher of the Hebrew tongue at Harvard, compiled the material for student use. Note the use of the Sephardic transliteration of Ivrit, above the title (American Jewish Historical Society)

arrival of Doctor Nuñez and family in London, the settlement of Georgia and the fine climate and soil of that country were the subjects of much speculation. The celebrated John Wesley and his brother Charles had resolved to embrace the occasion of visiting this El Dorado, and, when the ship which conveyed Governor Oglethorpe to that new settlement was about sailing, the doctor and his whole family embarked as passengers, not one of whom could speak the English language.

From *Statistics of Georgia,* by George White,
as quoted in *Publications of the American Jewish
Historical Society,* Vol. 2, 1894, pp. 46–47

A NEW YORK CONGREGATION
Engages a Hazan, 1757

One of the first acts of a Jewish community in the colonies was to buy a plot of ground for a cemetery. Their second institution was a synagogue. A school came next, as the only other education available was in Protestant schools.

Though synagogues were not permitted in New Amsterdam, worship was allowed in private homes. The Jews began private services as soon as they arrived in 1654.

When the British seized New Amsterdam in 1664, they granted freedom of conscience to Dutch Christians. The Jews petitioned several times for the right to establish a synagogue, and by 1685 they held semi-private services. A New York map of 1695 shows a "Jews' synagogue" with a congregation of twenty families, on Beaver Street.

The first synagogue in the colonies was Congregation Shearith Israel (Remnant of Israel) in New York, founded in 1710. (Minutes dated 1729 refer to a constitution as far back as 1706.) The Spanish-Portuguese Synagogue, as it is called, is still in existence and uses the Sephardic ritual. By the end of the century, all religious restrictions in New York had disappeared.

Other synagogues in pre-Revolutionary days arose in Savannah (1733), Charleston, S.C. (1750), and Newport, R.I. (1763).

It was not easy for these congregations to maintain themselves. Rabbis, cantors, and teachers had to be imported, but the tiny, struggling communities had little to offer in the way of pay. The first American-born "rabbi" was Gershom Mendez Seixas (1745–1816) who served Shearith Israel for forty-eight years.

The following correspondence shows the congregation's efforts to engage a *hazan* (cantor). The initials K.K. stand for *Kahal Kadosh* (Holy Congregation) and the transliteration reflects the Sephardic Hebrew pronunciation.

"... A Young Man of good Morals & strictly religious. ..."

MESSRS. THE Parnas & Gentlement in the Direction of the K.K. of Seerit Israel in New York:

London, October 28 of 1757 or 14th *Hesvan* 5518

Gentlemen,

We acknowledge the Receipt of your Favour of the 4th *Elul*, by the Hands of Mr. Moses Franks, whereby you desire us to recommend you a Young Man of good Morals & strictly religious, . . . of an agreable Voice & Capacity for teaching of Hebrew & translating it into English as well as Spanish, . . . in reading the Prayers & the Law, as also for instructing the poor Boys; . . . some have offered themselves, tho' not such as we could entirely wish, however . . . some one may appear, worthier of our Recommendation, but we foresee that who ever presents himself as a Candidate will insist that his Passage and Charges be defray'd & will expect that an Agreement be made for a certain Term of Years, since otherwise it will be very precarious for any Man to go over, liable to be displaced upon any Dislike; and exposed to return at his own Expence; Considering . . . we therefore hope to have in Time your further Instructions on the above, and whether a married Man with a Family would be approved of, as also whether the Fifty Pounds Sterling is exclusive of Offerings & Perquisites, for tho' these are voluntary and uncertain they still may serve as an Inducement to a Person properly qualified, who without such Encouragement may not think it expedient to go;

An old print of the Mill Street Synagogue, the first synagogue building of Congregation Shearith Israel, New York City. The congregation, the oldest in North America, was founded in 1710; the building, erected in 1729, was consecrated April 8, 1730. (American Jewish Archives)

Gershom Mendez Seixas (1745-1816), first American-born "rabbi," served Shearith Israel for forty-eight years. (American Jewish Archives)

We sincerely wish you, Prosperity & Happiness, and conclude subscribing ourselves:

Gentlemen

Your very humble Servants

The Parnassim & Gabay of the K.K. of Sahar Asamaim

Moses Lopes Pereira

Daniel Mendes Seixas

Moses Gomes Serra

Moseh De Jacob Franco

Hananel Mendes Da Costa, Gabay

✿   ✿   ✿   ✿   ✿

Messrs. The Parnassim and Gabay of the K.K. of Sahar Asamaim in London

New York, March 13th 1758 or 3d *Veadar* 5518

Gentlemen,

Wee have received the favour of your Letter of the 14th *Hesvan* whareby wee are Acquainted that No Suteable Person and Worthy of your recommendation had yet presented. . . . However, . . . wee have no Objection to a married man but would choose one, rather if with a Small Family . . . as our Congregation is Small and few that are Able To Contribute to the Support thereof The Salary of Fifty Pounds Sterling, is Exclusive of voluntary offerings, Marriages and other things of that Kind, also of those Children whose Parants are able to pay for thire Schoolinge, Should a proper Person present wee Shall defray the reasonable Expence of thire Sea Store and Passage . . . As to Settling a Salary for a term of years or Returning at our Expence, on any little Disquiet which he Might take, it is not agreable to the Congregation, and wee Presume might be attended with bad Consequence, . . . and be the very meanes of Producing Some kind of Dislike which wee would Willingly Avoid but wee think there will be no reason to doubt his Continuance Should he not Misbehave, which wee hope will Not happen as wee are Confident that your goodness would not Recommend any but

Such as may Appear proper & worthy Thereof, wee Shall Esteem the favour of your Answer Soon as possible, that if wee cant Soon have a proper Person from London on these terms, wee may Endeavor to provide for one Some other way wee Sincerely wish you all Prosperity and Happieness and Conclude with Due respect

> Gentlemen
> your most Obliged Hb Serv,
> The Parnassim and Elders in the Direction
> of the K K. of Seherith Israel in New York.

✿   ✿   ✿   ✿   ✿

> New York, March 13th—1758

Mr. Moses Franks

Sir,

Wee Acknowledge our Selves Indebted to you for your favr, & Deligence in waiting on the Gentm of the *Mahamad* with our Letter . . . Imboldens us to Intrude further on your goodness Desiring youl be so Kind to Deliver the Inclosd, being an Answer to thire Letter Should they Nominate any Person Worthy of Thire Recomandation to Come over in the Carictor of a *Hazan* for our Congregation, Desire youl be pleasd, to Supply him with as much as may be reasonable to lay in a deceant Sea Store & Pay the passages Should he be a man with a family . . . for which you may Draw on us or Shall order the payment at London as it Sutes best your Assistance thirein may get thire passage at a more moderate Rate . . . wee Conclude wishing you a Merry Holyday, with health & prosperity, wee are Respectfully

> Sir yor Fd & most Humble Servt—
> I G
> S S

From *Publications of the American Jewish Historical Society,* Vol. 27, 1920, pp. 8–11

NEW YORK JEWS Respond to an Appeal from Safed, 1761

In an age when there was no telegraphy, radio, or fast postal service, the Jews throughout the world—then numbering perhaps two million—managed to keep in touch with each other, no matter how widely they were scattered.

Their contacts with other Jews were a life line. To whom else could they turn in time of need or trouble? Whom could they count on, alone as they always were, outnumbered in a hostile world? They relied mainly on trusted emissaries who often would travel long and dangerous distances to carry a message between far-flung communities.

In 1761 a cry for help reached the Jews in New York City. It had traveled 6,000 miles from the town of Safed in Palestine to the New World. The Jewish community of the ancient holy city of Safed had been devastated by the terrible earthquake of 1760.

The appeal for help for the survivors came to Congregation Shearith Israel.

How the Jews reached each other, their system of emissaries, and how they rallied to the assistance of their distant brethren in trouble are seen in the touching letters that follow. The first was written in Portuguese, the second in Spanish.

———

"We pledge ourselves as sponsors for this mitzvah. . . ."

London Feb. 17 [61]

F ROM THE enclosed letters of the very Reverend Haham [Chief Rabbi] Haim Mudahy . . . , you will learn of the wretched and deplorable condition of our poor brethren in that part of the world. . . . We . . . know of their great misfortune and of the necessity for immediate relief. We pledge ourselves as sponsors for this *mitzvah* [good deed] and are sure that the Congregation will not only contribute as a whole but that each individual member will give generously toward the relief of that poor *Kehilah* [community] which has suffered so much . . . [and] to reestablish the destroyed synagogues and the ruined *medrasim* [houses of study]. May the Almighty influence your hearts and endow us with the will to do good. May He deliver you from similar misfortunes and grant you many years.

Your sincere servants
Manasseh Mendes da Costa
Ephraim de Aquilar

❀   ❀   ❀   ❀   ❀

". . . One hundred and sixty souls lie
buried beneath the ruins. . . ."

Illustrious Gentlemen, the Parnassim, Gabayim, and other Gentlemen of the Kehilah Kadosh of New York, which God may increase and prosper.

I humbly and respectfully beg to state that, from the accompanying letters written to you by my companions appointed from the Holy Land and who are now in Constantinople, you will learn of the great misfortune and calamity which our brethren have suffered in the holy city of Zaphet [Safed] caused by the earthquake . . . on the 9th of *Hesvan* of the year 5520 [October 30, 1760]. The earthquake damaged the synagogues as well as the large *Midrash;* many houses were totally destroyed and many people lost all they possessed. They were obliged to flee from their homes in their shirts . . . and one hundred and sixty souls lie buried beneath the ruins, their own homes being their tombs.

This misfortune plunged the city into great distress and . . . forced the above-mentioned gentlemen to send a representative in order to call the attention of other holy and charitable *Kehilot* to the necessity for prompt and liberal relief to alleviate the . . . terrible misfortune and unspeakable distress. . . .

This committee of the Holy Land selected me to go to all the *Kehilot* for relief funds. Though this journey necessitated my leaving my work as one of the *Dayanim* [judges] of the holy *Kehilah* of Constantinople and meant that I give up the continuous study of the Holy Law, I could not refuse so urgent a mission. . . . Divine Providence has assisted me for . . . there is not a Congregation, no matter how small, in Italy, France, and . . . in Amsterdam, which has not contributed generously. . . .

I trust to Divine Grace that you will undertake the work with all your hearts . . . and that you will gladly contribute as generously . . . as have other *Kehilot,* so that, by your acts, Omnipotent God may redeem us from our bitter and prolonged captivity; and [that] He may bless you, prosper and increase you. I salute you from the depths of my heart. . . .

Your most humble and sincere servant

Haim Mudahy

From *Publications of the American Jewish Historical Society,* Vol. 27, 1920, pp. 18–20

MOSES MICHAEL HAYS Protests a Loyalty Oath, 1776

When the American colonies rebelled against England, not all their citizens supported the Revolution.

The majority were indifferent. About a third were Tories (mainly the prosperous and conservative aristocracy) or Loyalists, faithful to the Crown. The Whigs (the liberals) called themselves Patriots. Most Jews fell into the Patriot camp.

The Patriots, trying to organize the Revolution, regarded the Loyalists as self-serving enemies, and feeling against them ran high. Threats, vilification, rumor, and suspicion often exploded into violence.

In June, 1776, the Rhode Island Assembly passed an act requiring a loyalty oath (or test) to the Revolutionary cause. After the Declaration of Independence, it punished anyone who recognized the British king. Promptly, officers of the Rhode Island Brigade named sixty-seven Newportians as "inimical to the united colonies." Among them were four Jews.

Humiliated and smarting at the injustice, the Jews refused to sign the loyalty test—an act of courage in that time of mounting patriotic hysteria. One of the four was Rabbi Isaac de Touro of Congregation Jeshuat Israel. Another was native-born Moses Michael Hays of a distinguished Revolutionary family. In this selection, Hays (who had signed the test in June) explains his refusal. (We note that Jews still could not vote in Rhode Island; they had been refused naturalization in 1761.) Later, Hays requested an investigation so as to obtain full vindication.

In later years Hays became a leading citizen of Boston (though his was the only Jewish family there), highly respected by his Yankee neighbors. He was elected grand master of the Grand Lodge of Masons of Massachusetts with Paul Revere under him as his deputy grand master. He helped found one of the first banks in America, the bank of Massachusetts.

"Second, . . . I am an Israelite and am not allowed the liberty of a vote. . . ."

HE REFUSED to sign the Test and called for his accusers. He was then told there was a number present whom he there saw. He likewise called for his accusation which was read: "I have and ever shall hold the strongest principles and attachments to the just rights and privileges of this my native land and ever have and shall conform to the rules and acts of this government and pay as I always have my proportion of its exigencies. I always have asserted my sentiments in favor of America and confess the War on its part just. I decline subscribing the Test at present from these principles, first, that I deny ever being inimical to my country and call for my accusers and proof of conviction; second, that I am an Israelite and am not allowed the liberty of a vote or voice in common with the rest of the voters though consistent with the Constitution and the other Colonies; thirdly, because the Test is not general and consequently subject to many glaring inconveniences; fourthly, Continental Congress nor the General Assembly of this nor the Legislatures of the other Colonies have never in this contest taken any notice or countenance respecting the society of Israelites to which I belong. When any rule order or directions is made by the Congress or General Assembly I shall to the utmost of my power adhere to the same."

From the *Rhode Island Archives*
General Assembly Papers, Revolutionary War,
Suspected Persons, 1775–1783, p. 16

MORDECAI SHEFTALL Recalls
His Capture by the British, 1778

"Born an aristocrat, he became a democrat;
An Englishman, he cast his lot with America;
True to his ancient faith, he gave his life
For new hopes of human liberty and understanding."

These words are inscribed on the marker on the grave of Francis Salvador (1747–1776), the first Jew in South Carolina to hold public office and the first to die for American independence.

He was not the only Jew to lay down his life for the American cause. Lewis Bush, captain of the Sixth Pennsylvania Battalion, died of wounds received in the battle of Brandywine. Joseph Solomon of South Carolina fell in the battle of Beaufort, 1779.

Records have come down to us of over one hundred Jews who fought in the Continental armies—a high percentage since the Jews were barely 2,000 in a total population of 2,000,000. Many became officers, for the Jewish colonists were on the whole well educated. At least four rose to the rank of colonel.

One of them was Solomon Bush who was luckier than his relative Lewis. An officer in the Pennsylvania Militia for ten years, he was seriously wounded in battle but survived to become lieutenant colonel.

Another, Isaac Franks (1759–1822) of the well-known Franks family, was only seventeen when he enlisted in the New York Volunteers and fought in the battle of Long Island. Imprisoned when New York was captured, he escaped and continued to serve, ending up as lieutenant colonel of the Eighth Regiment of the Pennsylvania County Brigade. A personal friend of many notables, he was host to President Washington at his house in Germantown during a yellow fever epidemic in 1793. The noted painter Gilbert Stuart, Franks's good friend, painted a famous portrait of him.

A Colonel Isaacs of the North Carolina Militia is mentioned as wounded and taken prisoner in Camden, N.C., in 1780 and later exchanged.

Benjamin Nones had barely arrived from Bordeaux, France, when he enlisted. He served under Count Pulaski in the siege of Savannah and received a certificate for gallant conduct on the field of battle. He ended up a major.

Three (possibly four) Pinto brothers, of an old Connecticut family, were active in the Revolution—Abraham, William (who may not have been a brother), Jacob, and Solomon (wounded in the British attack on New Haven, 1779).

Meanwhile, in the New Jersey troops there fought a young man named Asher Levy—grandson of the Asser Levy who stood up to Peter Stuyvesant in New Amsterdam.

One company of the South Carolina Militia was referred to as "the Jewish regiment" because forty of its sixty members were Jews.

What an array of legendary names comes to life in the records of other Jewish soldiers! We read of Jacob de la Motta and Jacob de Leon, captains under General de Kalb; of Nathaniel Levy of Baltimore who fought under Lafayette; of Manuel Mordecai Noah (1747–1825) who served under General Marion; of Captain Noah Abraham with the battalion of Cumberland City militia of Pennsylvania; of Aaron Benjamin who rose to regimental adjutant of the Eighth Connecticut Regiment; of Isaac Israel, a captain in the Eighth Virginia Regiment.

Sometimes we learn indirectly of a Jewish soldier. Thus we find record of one Hart Jacobs in New York who was exempted from military duty on Friday night because it was the Jewish Sabbath.

Mordecai Sheftall (1735–1797) has left us an account of what it meant to be a British prisoner. Sheftall, one of the first white children born in Georgia, was the son of a German settler who had arrived in 1733 (see selection 10). During the Revolution he was appointed commissary-general of the Georgia troops and then deputy commissary of issues in South Carolina and Georgia. He was captured when Savannah was taken by the British. His first-hand account of that experience follows.

In 1782 Sheftall turned up in Philadelphia where many Patriot refugees found haven. Like the Gratzes and the Frankses, he was one of the German founders of the Sephardic synagogue, Mikveh Israel (Hope of Israel).

". . . I suffered a great deal of abuse and was threatened to be run through the body. . . ."

THIS DAY the British troops, consisting of about three thousand five hundred men, including two battalions of Hessians, under the command of Lieutenant Colonel Archibald Campbell, of the 71st Regiment of [Scottish] Highlanders, landed . . . at Brewton Hill, two miles below the town of Savannah. . . . At about three o'clock P.M., they . . . took possession of Savannah, when I endeavoured, with my son Sheftall, to make our escape across Musgrove Creek . . . but after having sustained a very heavy fire of musketry from the light infantry . . . we found it high water; . . . and we, with about one hundred and eighty-six officers and privates, being caught, as it were, in a pen, and the Highlanders keeping up a constant fire on us, it was thought advisable to surrender ourselves prisoners, which . . . was no sooner done than the Highlanders plundered every one amongst us. . . . We were all marched to the court-house which was very much crowded. . . . Major Crystie called for me by name and ordered me to follow him, which I did, with my blanket and shirt under my arm, my clothing and my son's . . . having been taken from my horse, so that my wardrobe consisted of what I had on my back.

The Mirwot for opening the ה"ר, Zemirot, Kadish, & Aftora
for Sabbath ^to be publish'd — & begin the Prayers for Sabbath as usual,
the Congregation to be particularly carefull not to
raise their Voices higher than the Hazan's, who will
endeavor to modulate his Voice to a proper Pitch
so as only to fill the Building —

His Excellency the President, & Honble Delegates of the United States הנתן ונ׳
of America in Congress Assembled — His Excellency George Washington
Captain General & Commander in Chief of the federal Army of these
States, His Excellency the President, the Honble Executive Council
& Members of the General Assembly of this Commonwealth, & all Kings
& Potentates in Alliance with North America: מלך מלכי ונ׳

מי שביריך וג׳ את כל הקק הזה מקוה ישראל פוה קדשים ותנוכה ה׳ שנדבו רוחם
לקנות הקרקע ולדנות עליו בית הכנסת הזאת / שכוחנו מהנבי׳ ומקד ש׳ה׳יום
לעצודת ה׳ אלקיע דאו ... את ה׳ אלקי מלכם דעולים ונ׳

בסימן טוב ... מצני הכנות לסוד בית הכנסת הזאת
מי שביריך ...

שקבע את הכלבנים תחת המוזוות בסן צבינהט והלבן
the first three named are deburnt ... הרשום 33 בית הכנסת הזאת

שריבנו את העמודם בבית הכנסת הזאת
except J. M. Levy, one is dead, & the
rest are now married Men

*The order of service for the dedication of Congregation Mikveh
Israel of Philadelphia, 1782, included a prayer for George Washington. (American Jewish Historical Society)*

On the way to the white guard-house we met with Colonel Campbell who . . . desired that I might be well guarded as I was a very great rebel. The major . . . ordered the sentry to guard me with a drawn bayonet and not to suffer me to go without the reach of it; . . . until a Mr. Gild Busler, their commissary general, ordered me to go with him to my stores that he might get some provisions for our people who, he said, were starving, having eat nothing for three days, which I contradicted, as I had victualized them that morning. . . . He ordered me to give him information of what stores I had in town and what I had sent out of town and where. This I declined doing, which made him angry. He asked me if I knew Charleston was taken. I told him no. He then called us poor, deluded wretches and said, "Good God! how are you deluded by your leaders!" When I inquired of him who had taken it and when, he said General Grant . . . eight or ten days ago; I smiled and told him it was not so, as I had a letter . . . that was wrote three days ago by my brother. He replied, we had been misinformed. I then retorted that I found they could be misinformed by their leaders as well as we . . . by ours. This made him so angry that . . . he ordered me to be confined amongst the drunken soldiers and Negroes, where I suffered a great deal of abuse and was threatened to be run through the body or, as they termed it, skivered by one of the York Volunteers, which he attempted . . . three times during the night but was prevented by one Sergeant Campbell.

In this situation I remained two days without a morsel to eat, when a Hessian officer named Zaltman, finding I could talk his language, removed me to his room and sympathized with me. . . . He permitted me to send to Mrs. Minis who sent me some victuals. He also permitted me to see my son and to let him stay with me. He introduced me to Captain Kappel, also a Hessian, who treated me very politely. In this situation I remained until . . . the 2nd of January, 1779, when the commander, Colonel Innis, sent . . . for me and son. . . . I met with Captain Stanhope, of the Raven sloop of war, who treated me with the most illiberal abuse and . . . ordered me on board the prison-ship, together with my son. I made a point of giving Mr. Stanhope suitable answers to his impertinent treatment and then . . . inquired for Colonel Innis. I got his leave to go to Mrs. Minis for a shirt she had taken to wash for me, as it was the only one I had left, except the one on my back and that was given me by Captain Kappel. . . . This favour he granted me under guard; after which I was . . . put on board the prison-ship Nancy . . . when the first thing that presented itself to my view was one of our poor continental soldiers laying on the ship's main deck in the agonies of death and who expired in a few hours after. After being presented to the captain . . . , I gave him in charge what paper money I had and my watch. . . . He appeared to be a little civiller after this confidence placed in him. . . . In the evening we were served with what was called our allowance which consisted of two pints and a half, and a half-gill of rice, and about seven ounce of boiled beef per man.

From *Historical Collections of Georgia*,
by George White, New York, 1855, pp. 340–342,
as quoted in *Publications of the American Jewish
Historical Society*, Vol. 17, 1909, pp. 176–178

JAMES MADISON Writes about Haym Salomon, 1782

The Jews threw all their resources into the Patriot cause.

Jewish importers signed the Non-Importation Resolutions, which meant they would not buy English goods. The gun factory of Joseph Simon and other Jewish gunsmiths began to turn out arms for Washington's armies. Jewish merchants and Indian traders provisioned the troops. Jewish officials assisted in movements of the army. Jewish-owned ships were converted into privateers.

Jews of any means contributed funds. Wealthier Jews extended credit for provisions for the army, often beyond their means, and became impoverished themselves. Among those who gave large sums were Mordecai Sheftall, David Salisbury Franks, Manuel Mordecai Noah, Benjamin Levy, Samuel Lyons, Isaac Moses, and Benjamin Jacobs.

But one man contributed more than all the others together—Polish-born Haym Salomon (1740–1784), a man of extraordinary talents who is called "the financier of the Revolution." When he arrived in New York about 1772, he lined up with the American cause. Risking his life in dangerous missions, he was arrested as a spy by the British; while imprisoned, he helped French and American prisoners to escape and talked some of the Hessians into deserting. He finally escaped to Philadelphia where his genius at finance soon became evident. Robert Morris (1734–1806), superintendent of finance for the young country, relied on him for many of his financial transactions, and Salomon helped prop up the government's shaky credit.

Salomon also advanced money to officers and officials

who were in financial straits in that difficult time. Without his help, many of them would have had to leave the public service.

Among those indebted to him were Thomas Jefferson and James Madison. Madison, then a delegate to the Continental Congress, later became the fourth president of the United States. In the following excerpts from his letters, Madison describes the generosity and tact of "our little friend in Front Street."

Morris's records show that Salomon contributed $350,000 to the United States government—a vast sum at that time. His heirs were never able to recover any of it nor even to obtain official recognition of their ancestor's services to his country.

". . . He obstinately rejects all recompense."

September 30, 1782

Dear Sir,

The letter from the Govr. to the Delegation recd. yesterday along with yours of the twentieth inst. . . .

The remittance to Col. Bland is a source of hope to his brethren. I am almost ashamed to reiterate my wants so incessantly to you, but they begin to be so urgent that it is impossible to suppress them. The kindness of our little friend in Front Street near the Coffee House is a fund which will preserve me from extremities, but I never resort to it without great mortification as he obstinately rejects all recompense. The price of money is so usurious that he thinks it ought to be extorted from none but those who aim at profitable speculations. To a necessitous Delegate he gratuitously spares a supply out of his private stock.

I conceive very readily the affliction & anguish which our friend at Monticello must experience at his irreparable loss. . . . Perhaps this domestic catastrophe may prove in its operation

ROBERT MORRIS · GEORGE WASHINGTON · HAYM SALOMON

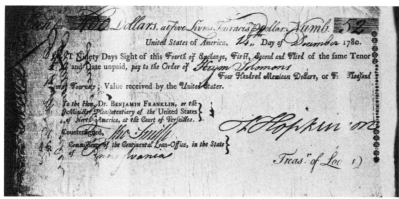

Top: Statue designed by American sculptor Lorado Taft. (American Jewish Archives)
Bottom: Facsimile of a promissory note issued to Haym Salomon by the United States government, 1780.

beneficial to his country by weaning him from those attachments which deprived it of his services. . . .

No addition has been made to our stock of intelligence from Europe since the arrival of the Frigates. Some letters from the Marquis de la Fayette & others have since come to hand but they are all of the same date. . . .

From a letter from James Madison to Edmund Randolph, in *The Papers of James Madison*, Volume V, edited by William Hutchison and William M. E. Rachal, University of Chicago Press, 1967, pp. 170–171

BENJAMIN RUSH Attends
a Jewish Wedding, 1787

A Jew was a strange and exotic creature to most Americans in the early days of the republic. With only about 2,000 Jews scattered throughout the states, many people had never seen one. It was with great interest, therefore, that Benjamin Rush accepted an invitation to a Jewish wedding in Philadelphia.

Dr. Rush (1745–1813), a distinguished American, *was* was one of the signers of the Declaration of Independence, A physician, he established America's first free dispensary, (Philadelphia, 1786). He was the father of Richard Rush, temporary U.S. secretary of state and a minister to Great Britain.

His host, Jonas Phillips (1736–1803), was also a striking personality. Originally from Germany, he came in 1756 to Charleston as an indentured servant to pay his passage. After serving his indenture he eventually moved to New York. He married a Sephardic girl, Rebecca Machado, although the aristocratic Sephardim (Spanish Jews) usually disdained Ashkenazim (German or Western Jews). He became a leading citizen of New York and, later, of Philadelphia. He founded a great clan, for his wife bore him twenty-one children.

The wedding united Phillips's daughter Rachel with Michael Levy of Virginia. An offspring of that union was Uriah Phillips Levy (1792–1862) who became a commodore in the United States Navy and abolished corporal punishment in the Navy. Another was Jonas Phillips Levy (1807–1883) who commanded the U.S.S. *America* in the Mexican War and, when Vera Cruz fell, was made captain of its port.

The following letter from Rush to his wife describes

the Phillips wedding. Like any warmhearted Jewish wife and mother, Mrs. Phillips sent a piece of wedding cake to Mrs. Rush.

"I was carried back to the ancient world. . . ."

Philadelphia, June 27, 1787

My dear Julia,

Being called a few days ago to attend in the family of Jonas Phillips, I was honored this morning with an invitation to attend the marriage of his daughter to a young man of the name of Levy from Virginia. . . . I accepted with great pleasure. . . .

At 1 o'clock the company, consisting of thirty or forty men, assembled in Mr. Phillips's common parlor which was accommodated with benches. . . . The ceremony began with prayers in the Hebrew language, chaunted by an old rabbi . . . followed by the whole company. As I did not understand a word except now and then an Amen or Hallelujah, my attention was directed to the haste with which they covered their heads with their hats as soon as the prayers began and to the freedom with which some of them conversed during . . . this part of their worship. As soon as these prayers were ended, . . . about twenty minutes, a small piece of parchment was produced, written in Hebrew, which contained a deed of settlement and which the groom subscribed in the presence of four witnesses. In this deed he conveyed a part of his fortune to his bride, by which she was provided for after his death. . . . This was followed by the erection of a beautiful canopy of white and red silk . . . supported by four young men (by means of four poles) who put on white gloves for the purpose. As soon as this canopy was fixed, the bride, accompanied with . . . a long train of female relations, came downstairs. Her face was covered with a veil which reached halfways down her body. She was handsome at all times, but the occasion and her dress rendered her . . . a most lovely and affecting object. . . . I gazed with delight upon her. Innocence, modesty, fear, respect, and devotion appeared all at once in her countenance. She was led by her two bridesmaids under the canopy. Two young men led the bridegroom . . . directly opposite to her. The priest now began again to chaunt an Hebrew prayer, . . . followed by part of the company. After this he gave to the groom and bride a glass full of wine, from which they each sipped. . . . Another prayer followed . . . after which he took a ring and directed the groom to place it upon the finger of his bride . . . as in the marriage service of the Church of England. This was followed by handing the wine to the father of the bride and then . . . to the bride and groom. The groom after sipping the wine took the glass . . . and threw it upon a large pewter dish which was suddenly placed at his feet. Upon its breaking into a number of small pieces, there was a general shout of joy and a declaration that the ceremony was over. The groom now saluted his bride, and kisses and congratulations became general. . . . I asked the meaning . . . of the canopy and of the wine and breaking of the glass. I was told . . . that in Europe they generally marry in the open air and that the canopy was introduced to defend the bride and groom from the . . . sun and from rain. . . . Partaking of the same glass of wine was intended to denote the mutuality of their goods, and the breaking of the glass . . . to teach them the brittleness and uncertainty of human life and the certainty of death, and thereby to temper their present joys.

Mr. Phillips pressed me to stay and dine with the company, but business . . . forbade it. I stayed, however, to eat some wedding cake and to drink a glass of wine. . . . Upon going . . . upstairs to ask how Mrs. Phillips did, who had fainted downstairs under pressure of the heat . . . , I discovered the bride and groom supping a bowl of broth together. Mrs. Phillips apologized for them by telling me they had eaten nothing (agreeably to the custom prescribed by their religion) since the night before.

Upon my taking leave, Mrs. Phillips put a large piece of cake into my pocket for you, which she begged I would present to you with her best compliments. . . .

During the whole of this new and curious scene . . . I was carried back to the ancient world and was led to contemplate the passovers, the sacrifices, the jubilees, and other ceremonies of the Jewish Church. After this, I . . . anticipated the time foretold by the prophets when this once-beloved race of men shall again be restored to the divine favor and shall unite with Christians . . . in celebrating the praises of a common and universal Saviour. . . .

Adieu. With love to your Mama, sisters, and brothers, and to our dear children, I am your affectionate husband,

B. Rush

P.S. . . . I have sent the wedding cake by Mr. Stockton.

From *The Letters of Benjamin Rush*, edited by L. H. Butterfield, 1951, pp. 429–432, as quoted in *Publications of the American Jewish Historical Society*, Vol. XLII, 1952–53, pp. 189–192

JONAS PHILLIPS Writes to the Federal Constitutional Convention, 1787

When the thirteen colonies had won their independence, they united as states under the Articles of Confederation. They soon found that the central government was too weak to be effective and that a constitution was necessary.

The Federal Constitutional Convention met in Philadelphia from May to September of 1787, George Washington presiding. Chief drafter of the new Constitution was James Madison.

The Jews in the United States, now numbering over 2,000, hoped the Constitution would guarantee their rights as full and equal citizens.

Jonas Phillips (whom we met in the preceding selection) took up the fight for Jewish rights begun by Asser Levy and others in the days of Peter Stuyvesant.

An ardent Patriot living in New York when independence was declared, he was one of those who moved to Philadelphia rather than remain under British rule. In 1773 he joined the Revolutionary Army, serving in the Philadelphia Militia under Colonel Bradford. A founder of Congregation Mikveh Israel, Philadelphia's Sephardic synagogue, he was its president when it was consecrated in 1782.

In the following letter to the Convention, Phillips writes vigorously in behalf of Jewish rights.

Actually, the Constitutional Convention had already adopted a clause barring any religious test for public office. But Jewish political participation varied in the states which were, in certain respects, still sovereign.

"By the above law a Jew is deprived of holding any publick office. . . ."

Sires,

With leave and submission I address myself to those in whom there is wisdom, understanding, and knowledge; they are the honourable personages appointed and Made overseer of . . . the thirteen united states of America in Convention Assembled, the Lord preserve them amen.—

I the subscriber, being one of the people called Jews of the City of Philadelphia, a people scattered & dispersed among all nations, do behold with Concern that, among the laws in the Constitution of Pennsylvania, there is a Clause Sect 10 to viz— "I do believe in one God the Creator and Governor of the universe the Rewarder of the good & the punisher of the wicked— and I do acknowledge the Scriptures of the old & new testament to be given by divine inspiration"—to swear & believe that the new testament was given by divine inspiration is absolutely against the Religious principle of a Jew and is against his Conscience to take any such oath—By the above law a Jew is deprived of holding any publick office . . . which is a Contradictory to the bill of Right Sect 2 viz

> —That all men have the natural and unalienable right to worship almighty God according to the dictates of their own conscience and understanding; and that no man ought or of right can be compelled to attend any religious worship, or erect or support any place of worship or maintain any minister contrary to or against his own free will and consent, nor can any man who acknowledges the being of a God be justly deprived or abridged of any civil right as a Citizen on account of his religious sentiments or peculiar mode of religious worship; and that no authority can or ought to be vested in or assumed by any power whatever that shall in any case interfere or in any manner controul

inspiration." To swear; believe that the new testament was given by divine inspiration, is absolutely against the religious principles of a Jew, and is against his conscience to take any such oath. By the above Law a Jew is deprived of holding any public Office or place of Government, which is contradictory to the bill of right, Sec. 2. Viz.

"That all men have the natural and unalianable right to worship almighty God according to the dictates of their own consciences and understanding; and that no man ought, or of right can be compelled to attend any religious worship, or erect or support any place of worship, or maintain any Minister, contrary to his own free will and consent; nor can any man who acknowledges the being of a God, be justly deprived or abridged of any civil right, as a Citizen, on account of his religious Sentiments or peculiar mode of religious worship; and that no authority can or ought to be vested in, or assumed by, any power whatever, that shall in any case interfere, or in any manner control, the right of conscience in the free exercise of religious worship."

It is well known among all the Citizens of the thirteen (13) United States, that the Jews have been true & faithful Whigs; and during the late Contest with England they have been foremost in aiding and assisting the States with their lives and fortunes; they

Segment of a letter from Jonas Phillips to the Federal Constitutional Convention on behalf of Jewish rights and religious equality. Note especially the portion indicated on the photograph. (American Jewish Historical Society) the right of conscience in the free exercise of religious worship.—

It is well known . . . that the Jews have been true and faithfull whigs, & during the late Contest with England they have been foremost in aiding and assisting the states with their lifes & fortunes, . . . have bravely fought and bled for liberty which they can not Enjoy.—

Therefore if the honourable Convention shall in their Wisdom think fit and alter the said oath & leave out the words to viz— "and I do acknowledge the Scripture of the new testament to be given by divine inspiration"—then the Israelites will think themself happy to live under a government where all Religious societys are on an Equal footing—I solicit this favour for myself my children & posterity, & for . . . all the Israelites through the thirteen united states of America.

My prayer is unto the Lord. May the people of this states Rise up as a great & young lion, May they prevail against their Enemies, may the degrees of honour of his Excellency the president of the Convention George Washington, be Exhalted & Raise up. . . .

May God prolong his days among us in this land of Liberty— May he lead the armies against his Enemys as he has done here-untofore. May God Extend peace unto the united states . . . so long as the sun & moon Endureth—and May the almighty God of our father Abraham Isaac & Jacob indue [endow?] this Noble Assembly with wisdom Judgment & unanimity in their Counsells & may they have the satisfaction to see that their present toil & labour for the wellfair of the united states may be approved of Through all the world & perticular by the united states of America, is the ardent prayer of, Sires,

Your Most devoted obed. Servant

Jonas Phillips

Philadelphia, 24*th Ellul* or *Sepr 7th* 1787

From *Publications of the American Jewish Historical Society*, Vol. 2, 1894, pp. 108–110

MANUEL JOSEPHSON Advises the Newport Congregation, 1790

It is hard to realize how far from Jewish practice some of the Jewish congregations in the colonies had drifted.

The letter which follows, from Manuel Josephson of Philadelphia to Moses Seixas of Newport, may prove a little startling: It reveals that the Newport congregation did not read the *Torah* at its services! In fact, the congregation did not seem to know that there was a "portion of the week" or to grasp that Josephson was not merely indulging in a pet preference of his own.

We must remember that most of the early settlers in America were Spanish and Portuguese, the descendants of Marranos who had not been able to practice their religion openly. They had been cut off from other Jewish congregations, the Hebrew language, and Jewish sources. Though they had tried to hold on to their Judaism, over the centuries they had lost more and more of what they dimly remembered.

Jeshuat Israel was almost entirely Sephardic, and its rabbis were lay people who had not been ordained. The United States did not have trained rabbis until the late nineteenth century when three theological schools were founded.

Ashkenazic Jews had started to emigrate to this country during the seventeenth century, and their numbers increased over the next hundred years. By the end of the eighteenth century they were a majority of the Jews in the United States. Philadelphia's Congregation Mikveh Israel (Hope of Israel) had been Sephardic at the start, but by the time its first synagogue was built in 1782 many of its leading members were German. One of the contributions of the German

Jews was their Jewish scholarship—their knowledge of Hebrew and of Jewish tradition.

Manuel Josephson, who answered Seixas's letter with courtesy and tact, was president of the Philadelphia synagogue. A prominent figure in Revolutionary annals, it was he who signed the letter from the Hebrew congregations of Philadelphia, New York, Richmond, and Charleston, December 13, 1790, congratulating George Washington on his presidency.

"... Essential and strictly commanded by our Laws. ..."

Philadelphia, 4th February 1790

Mr. Moses Seixas
Dear Sir,

On the 22ᵈ. Decemʳ. last I was favoured with your obliging Letter of 3ᵈ. of the same Month; to which for the want of Conveyance have not replied before. . . . You insinuate that to . . . alter your present Mode would be very impracticable or at best attended with much difficulty, having been adopted not from choice but necessity: nevertheless, if ye were convinced that what I advanced . . . was the result of Mature deliberation ye would one & all subscribe to my opinion; These Sentiments do me great honour and are highly flattering, especially in the polite manner you have conveyed them to me: I shall therefore endeavour to convince you that what I wrote is literally just & conformable to our Oral Law as deduced & digested from Scripture, and by no means matter of Opinion of my own. . . . But the case in question is distinctly to be found in all our Law Books of the first reputation. . . .

You say Mʳ. Rivera reads Hebrew perfectly, surely then it can't be so mighty a task for him to read from the *Sefer* [*Torah*] a few chapters occasionally; . . . he was bred to strict rules of Judaism and doubt not has imbibed the sentiment of his much respected and worthy Father of honoured Memory to keep up & support our holy religion & worship in every respect so much as possible—I therefore have no doubt that, on his being made acquainted with the preceding passages which shew that reading the *Parasah* [portion] from the *Sefer* [*Torah*] is essential & strictly commanded by our Laws, . . . he will not hesitate to perform that part of the service . . . ; or if that should not be agreeable to read the words altho without the *Ta'amim* [chanting] would still be preferable to your present mode. . . .

I duly observe what you are pleased to say, respecting the blowing of *Shofar* [ram's horn], your reasons for not performing that solemn & strictly enjoined service are beyond doubt of great weight; for there is no *Din* [ruling] to be found that insists on blowing a *Shofar* where there is none. . . . By your Letter it appears that you have instructed Mr. David Lopez Junr. to procure you one at Hamburg. . . . In the interim . . . I doubt not you might procure the Loan of one from New York. . . .

Your observations on the Blower you mention to have been at your place three years July . . . entirely justifies your being ashamed for the *Goyim* [non-Jews] but with this difference in your favour—that you were not ashamed of the performance but of the performer; and, if no other could be found than such a profligate as you describe him, I should not hesitate to suspend that part of the service for once, untill a person of good character would undertake to practice & perform; rather than have a Stigma cast on us & be derided not alone by *Goyim* but also by pious & well-thinking *Yehudim* [Jews]. . . .

. . . As no more room is left on the Paper must of necessity conclude with adding that Mrs. Josephson & our Niece return their best thanks for your friendly Salutation & offer theirs to your goodself, Mrs. Seixas, your good Mother, & rest of the Family and, believe me, with Sentiments of great regard—Dr. Sir yr esteemed friend & hum. Servt.

Manuel Josephson

From *Publications of the American Jewish Historical Society*, Vol. 27, 1920, pp. 185–190

NAPHTALI PHILLIPS Recalls the Federal Parade of 1788

By the end of 1788 enough states had ratified the new federal constitution to make it binding.

The milestone was celebrated with a parade by the Federalists in Philadelphia on July 4, 1788.

Naphtali Phillips (1773–1870) was fifteen years old when he took part in the parade, but he remembered it vividly all his days. Eighty years later he described it in detail in a letter to an old friend. The "kind, good parents" to whom he refers in his eyewitness account were none other than Jonas and Rebecca Phillips (see selections 16 and 17).

Naphtali Phillips became a leading citizen of New York City where he published a newspaper called *The National Advocate* and served as president of Congregation Shearith Israel. Married twice (to Rachel Mendez Seixas of Newport in 1797 and to Esther Mendez Seixas in 1823), he was the father of at least eight children (several are unrecorded), doing his share toward the growth of the great Phillips clan. Many other members of the family attained high stature in their communities: They included a surgeon, two dramatists, several leading lawyers, and high naval officers; a number held political office.

Naphtali Phillips's letter, which follows, shows a charm and courtly grace and is revealing of the modes and manners of its era. It is also known that a special kosher table had been prepared for the Jews who participated in the parade.

"... Holding in his hand the new Constitution in a frame."

New York, October 24th, 1868

My dear friend McAllister:

   ... As ... respects the great federal procession in "1788," I have been anticipated by the *Sunday Dispatch*. I shall make a few particulars in addition thereto.

First, in an open carriage drawn by elegant horses, sat Chief Justice McKane [Thomas McKean] with other judges of the [Pennsylvania] Supreme Court, holding in his hand the new Constitution in a frame. This was received by the populace with great rejoicing. ... Then came farmers with large cattle and sheep on a platform drawn by horses all handsomely decorated. The farmers were sowing grain as they walked along. Then came an handsome ship elegantly adorned with flags ..., manned by young mid-shipmen and drawn by horses, on wheels, and one of the crew throwing the lead as they passed along singing out in true sailors' voice. ...

Next, a printing press on a platform drawn by horses, compositors setting types; and the press worked by journeymen distributing some printed matter as they went along.

Speaking of the press brings to my mind the words of "Junius," as follows: "Let it be impressed on your minds, let it be instilled to your children that the liberty of the press is a great palladium of your civil and religious rights." ...

Next came blacksmiths with their forge, with a large bellows keeping up a blast to keep alive the flame of liberty. Next came shoemakers on a platform, men and boys soleing and heeltapping, others making wax ends. Then followed three fine-looking men dressed in black velvet, with large wigs on, densely powdered, representing the hairdressing society. Then the various trades followed with their appropriate insignia; young lads from different schools lead by their ministers and teachers, of which I was one of the boys.

The procession then proceeded . . . towards Bush Hill where there was a number of long tables loaded with all kinds of provisions, with a separate table for the Jews who could not partake of the meals from the other tables; but they had a full supply of soused [pickled] salmon, bread and crackers, almonds, raisins, etc. This table was under the charge of an old cobbler named Isaac Moses, well known in Philadelphia at that time. There was no spirituous liquor. . . . Having doon [done] full justice to the good things provided for, the procession then retrograded. . . .

I reached home late in the afternoon, fatigued and hungry. My kind, good parents having provided a good meal for me, I retired. . . .

Some time after the procession, a large sign was exhibited at some public house representing the Federal Convention members, . . . as they sat with Gen'l Washington at their head as their president, and . . . these words: "These thirty-seven great men together have agreed that better times shall soon succeed." . . .

When you see that *young* lady, Miss Ellet, make my best respects to her. . . . I shall have the honor to solicit her hand at . . . the next ball given in her honor, in dancing a minuet, as was the fashion in the olden times when we went to balls, when the city lamps were lit, and [we] were all snug at home before eleven. It was then customary to see your partner safe at home and to call next morning to inquire of her health after the fatigue of the preceding evening. The lady was waiting for her partner and, after setting some time, if his company had been very agreeable, this led to an extensive acquaintance which sometimes ended in matrimonial co-partnership.

A few days ago I entered my ninety-sixth year. Ladies and gentlemen came to congratulate me . . . with a good sprinkling of children, grandchildren, and great-grandchildren, their ages ranging from seventy years to one week. . . .

I would have been very happy if you had been here to make one of the company, to hobnob with me in a glass of champagne or sherry. . . . My best regards to your honored father, with kind remembrance to those who may inquire after me, and believe me, my dear friend, to be your sincere friend.

Naphtali Phillips

PS. More anon.

From American Jewish Archives,
January, 1955, pp. 65–67

EMMA LAZARUS Visits the Newport Synagogue, Abandoned in 1791

Today the old Jewish cemetery at Newport, Rhode Island, stands deserted. For a century—from 1677 to the Revolution—it served a thriving Jewish community that came from many directions, hopeful for Roger Williams's religious tolerance.

Fifteen Jewish families who came from Holland in 1658 probably found Jews from New Amsterdam and from Curaçao already there. Petitioning the Rhode Island General Assembly for permission to settle, they were promised "as good protection as any stranger ought to have . . . being obedient to His Majesty's laws." More Jews arrived from the West Indies in 1694 and, soon after, from Germany and Poland.

Newport already surpassed New York as a commercial center and port of entry. Its prosperity zoomed with an influx of enterprising Portuguese Jews, 1740 to 1750. Prominent and highly respected were Jacob Roderigues-Rivera, who built the sperm oil industry, and the cultured and urbane Aaron Lopez, who became the great merchant prince of New England. Two decades later, Newport had one hundred and fifty vessels in the West Indies trade alone. By the Revolution, Lopez himself owned thirty ships.

Religious services were held in private homes until 1763 when a synagogue was completed. The Touro Synagogue, so called after its rabbi Isaac Touro, is now a national monument.

The synagogue was closed at the outbreak of the Revolution when the British occupied Newport, December of 1776. The Jews, most of them supporters of

Touro Synagogue, Newport, Rhode Island. The synagogue is now a national monument. (Society of Friends of Touro Synagogue)

the Patriot cause, lost their property and had to flee. Many returned after the war. However, the town never regained its commercial importance, and they drifted off to Philadelphia, New York, Savannah, and Charleston. After 1791, the Touro Synagogue was closed for some sixty years.

A poem by Henry Wadsworth Longfellow has immortalized the ancient cemetery where many of the wanderers now lie at rest. A poem by Emma Lazarus, reproduced here, helps immortalize the synagogue.

"A man who reads the great God's written law. . . ."

In the Jewish Synagogue in Newport

Here, where the noises of the busy town,
    The ocean's plunge and roar can enter not,
We stand and gaze around with tearful awe,
    And muse upon the consecrated spot.

No signs of life are here: the very prayers
    Inscribed around are in a language dead;
The light of the "perpetual lamp" is spent
    That an undying radiance was to shed.

What prayers were in this temple offered up,
    Wrung from sad hearts, that knew no joy on earth,
By these lone exiles of a thousand years,
    From the fair sunrise land that gave them birth!

Now as we gaze, in this new world of light
    Upon this relic of the days of old,
The present vanishes, and tropic bloom
    And eastern towns and temples we behold.

Again we see the patriarch with his flocks,
　　The purple seas, the hot blue sky o'erhead,
The slaves of Egypt,—omens, mysteries,—
　　Dark fleeing hosts by flaming angels led.

A wondrous light upon a sky-kissed mount,
　　A man who reads the great God's written law,
'Midst blinding glory and effulgence rare
　　Unto a people prone with reverent awe.

The pride of luxury's barbaric pomp,
　　In the rich court of royal Solomon—
Alas! we wake: one scene alone remains,—
　　The exiles by the streams of Babylon.

Our softened voices send us back again
　　But mournful echoes through the empty hall;
Our footsteps have a strange unnatural sound,
　　And with unwonted gentleness they fall.

The weary ones, the sad, the suffering,
　　All found their comfort in the holy place,
And children's gladness and men's gratitude
　　Took voice and mingled in the chant of praise.

The funeral and the marriage, now, alas!
　　We know not which is sadder to recall;
For youth and happiness have followed age,
　　And green grass lieth gently over all.

Nathless the sacred shrine is holy yet,
　　With its lone floors where reverent feet once trod
Take off your shoes, as by the burning bush,
　　Before the mystery of death and God.

By Emma Lazarus

A GERMAN JEWISH SETTLER
Writes about Life in Virginia, 1792

When a young German Jewish couple settled in Virginia shortly after the Revolution, they were not worried about the hardships of pioneer life. What troubled them was the problem of rearing their two children in a small town with no Jewish community.

We know there were Jews in Virginia as early as 1624 because three are mentioned in the colony's early records. Two Virginia Jews, Michael Frank and Jacob Myer, received rewards for gallant services in Washington's 1754 expedition across the Alleghenies. The state's oldest synagogue, Congregation Beth-Sholom (House of Peace) in Richmond, dates before 1790.

But the young Jewish family looked longingly at Charleston, South Carolina's chief city, with its three hundred Jews and two synagogues. (The first Reform Jewish services were held in Charleston in 1824.) South Carolina had attracted Jewish settlers since its founding in 1670 because its charter (drawn up by British philosopher John Locke) granted freedom of conscience to all, including "Jews, Heretics, and Dissenters."

In 1740–1741, more Jews flocked to Charleston from Georgia which had adopted illiberal policies. Charleston's first synagogue, Congregation Beth Elohim (House of God), was founded by Portuguese Jews in 1750. The German Jews soon started their own synagogue as the Sephardic ritual was unfamiliar to them.

Commercial opportunities in the South drew Jews from New York to Charleston which by 1816 had the largest Jewish population of any United States city—

six hundred Jews. Some of them, like Dr. Levy Myers who became apothecary general of the state in 1796, rose to high office.

Charleston's Jewry maintained its leadership until it was impoverished and decimated by the Civil War.

In the letter that follows, the young wife tells her family in Germany what it meant to live in Petersburg, Virginia.

". . . In our house we all live as Jews as much as we can."

Dear Parents:

I hope my letter will ease your mind. You can now be reassured and send me one of the family to Charleston, South Carolina. This is the place to which, with God's help, we will go after Passover. The whole reason why we are leaving this place is because of [lack of] *Yehudishkeit* [Jewishness].

Dear parents, I know quite well you will not want me to bring up my children like Gentiles. Here they cannot become anything else. . . . There are here (in Petersburg) ten or twelve Jews, and they are not worthy of being called Jews. We have a *shochet* [ritual slaughterer] here who goes to market and buys *terefah* [nonkosher] meat and then brings it home. On *Rosh Hashanah* [the New Year] and on *Yom Kippur* [the Day of Atonement], the people worshipped here without one *sefer torah* [Scroll of the Law], and not one wore the *talit* [prayer shawl] or the *arba kanfot* [fringes worn on the body], except Hyman and my Sammy's godfather. The latter is an old man of sixty, a man from Holland. He has been in America for thirty years already. . . . He does not want to remain here any longer and will go with us to Charleston. In that place there is a blessed community of three hundred Jews.

You can believe me that I crave to see a synagogue to which I can go. The way we live now is no life at all. We do not know

Drawing of the synagogue of Charleston, South Carolina, by Solomon N. Carvalho. Congregation Beth Elohim was founded by Portuguese Jews in 1750. The synagogue was erected in 1795. (American Jewish Archives)

what the Sabbath and the holidays are. On the Sabbath, all the Jewish shops are open. . . . But ours we do not allow to open. With us there is still some Sabbath. You must believe me that in our house we all live as Jews as much as we can.

As for the Gentiles [?], we have nothing to complain about. For the sake of a livelihood we do not have to leave here. . . . I believe ever since Hyman has grown up that he has not had it so good. You cannot know what a wonderful country this is for the common man. One can live here peacefully. Hyman made a clock that goes very accurately, just like the one in the Buchenstrasse in Hamburg. Now you can imagine what honors Hyman has been getting here. In all Virginia there is no clock [like it], and Virginia is the greatest province in the whole of America, and America is the largest section of the world. Now you know what sort of a country this is. It is not too long since Virginia was discovered. It is a young country. And it is amazing to see the business they do in this little Petersburg. At times as many as a thousand hogsheads of tobacco arrive . . . and each hogshead contains 1,000 and sometimes 1,200 pounds of tobacco. The tobacco is shipped from here to the whole world.

When Judah [brother?] comes here, he can become a watchmaker and a goldsmith if he so desires. Here it is not like Germany where a watchmaker is not permitted to sell silverware. . . . They expect a watchmaker to be a silversmith here. Hyman . . . has a journeyman, a silversmith, a very good artisan, and he, Hyman, takes care of the watches. This work is well paid here, but in Charleston it pays even better.

All the people who hear that we are leaving give us their blessings. They say that it is sinful that such blessed children should be brought up here in Petersburg. My children cannot learn anything here, nothing Jewish, nothing of general culture. My Schoene [my daughter], God bless her, is already three years old. I think it is time that she should learn something, and she has a good head to learn. I have taught her bedtime prayers and grace after meals in just two lessons. . . . And my Sammy (born in 1790), God bless him, is already beginning to talk.

I could write more. However, I do not have any more paper.
I remain your devoted daughter and servant,
Rebecca, the wife of Hayyim, the son of Samuel the Levite,
I send my family, my . . . [mother-in-law?], and all my . . . good friends, my regards.

[Postscript:]

I, Hayyim, send my regards to you both and all my good friends. I do not have any time to write much. We shall, however, write another letter to you soon. . . . I should write to Raphael and my nephew. In the first place, they defamed me innocently, and, if they don't write to me first, I can assure them they will receive none from me; they will perhaps say they are not interested in me. I say the same thing. Further, I remain your devoted son,

The humble Hayyim, the son of Samuel, of blessed memory
From *American Jewry—Documents—Eighteenth Century,*
by Jacob R. Marcus, 1959, pp. 52–54

JOHN TRUMBULL Tells How David Franks Came to His Defense, 1793

One evening in 1793, Thomas Jefferson, secretary of state of the young United States of America, invited a few friends to dinner at his home. Among them was the noted historical painter John Trumbull (1756–1843) whose canvases, *The Signing of the Declaration of Independence* among others, hang in the Capitol in Washington.

Present also were Senator William B. Giles of Virginia and David Salisbury Franks who had come from England to Canada in 1774. He had had a glittering career in the United States Army.

Thomas Jefferson was reputed to be a Deist (one who believes in God but not in formal religion). When Trumbull was twitted by the others for his Christian beliefs, the only one to defend him was Franks, a practicing Jew (formerly president of the synagogue in Montreal).

Sympathetic to the Revolution, Franks had helped supply General Montgomery's army in Montreal and left with it when it retreated. He joined the Massachusetts Regiment and then served under Count d'Estaing, commander of the U.S. sea forces (1778). Later he was aide-de-camp to Benedict Arnold, but he was completely exonerated in the latter's treason trial (1780). After diplomatic missions for the Continental Congress in Paris, Madrid, Marseilles, and Morocco, he wound up as a lieutenant colonel. He had served the states from 1775–1786 without pay of any kind, ending up—like many other Jews who gave unstintingly—totally impoverished. In 1789 he was granted

David Salis-bury Franks, American patriot and soldier in the American Revolutionary War. (American Jewish Archives)

four hundred acres of land in recognition of his services during the war.

The incident recounted here by Trumbull gives a glimpse of Thomas Jefferson, the man who became our third president. We see that the Jew who had shared in the struggle for independence was accepted into the nation's highest social circles—in keeping with principles of the Declaration of Independence and of the Constitution.

The fact also reflects something of capitalism: In the first purely capitalistic country (without holdovers from feudalism, state religion, guilds, and a land-obsessed peasantry), a man's ability and achievement counted more than his religion.

"... And not a person to aid in my defense but my friend Mr. Franks who is himself a Jew."

I WAS scarcely seated when he (Giles) began to rally me on the puritanical ancestry and character of New England. I saw there was no other person from New England present, and, therefore, although conscious that I was in no degree qualified to manage a religious discussion, I felt myself bound to defend my country on this delicate point as well as I could. Whether it had been pre-arranged that a debate on the Christian religion, in which it should be powerfully ridiculed on the one side and weakly defended on the other, was to be brought forward as promising amusement to a rather free-thinking dinner party, I will not presume to say, but it had that appearance, and Mr. Giles pushed his raillery, to my no small annoyance, if not to my discomfiture, until dinner was announced. That I hoped would relieve me by giving a new turn to the conversation, but the company was hardly seated at table when he renewed the assault with increased asperity and proceeded so far at last as to ridicule the character, conduct, and doctrines of the divine Founder of our religion; Mr. Jefferson in the meantime smiling and nodding approval on Mr. Giles, while the rest of the company silently left me and my defense to our fate, until at length my friend David Franks took up the argument on my side. . . . I turned to Mr. Jefferson and said, "Sir, this is a strange situation in which I find myself; in a country professing Christianity and at a table with Christians, as I supposed, I find my religion and myself attacked with severe and almost irresistible wit and raillery and not a person to aid in my defense but my friend Mr. Franks who is himself a Jew."

From an autobiography by John Trumbull,
as quoted in *Jewish Life in New York before 1800*,
by Max James Kohler, pp. 92–93

UNION EDUCATION SERIES

EDITED BY

DANIEL B. SYME, *Acting Director*

Director of Publications
RALPH DAVIS

Editor of Keeping Posted
EDITH SAMUEL